ALABASTER

Alabaster Co. The Bible Beautiful.
Visual imagery & thoughtful design integrated within the Bible.
Cultivating conversation between art, beauty, & faith.

Founded in 2016.

NLT.

ARTIST INTRODUCTION

———

The Book of Isaiah comes at a troubled but pivotal time in Israel's history, recording the relationship between God and the Israelites during their downfall at the hands of the Assyrians and Babylonians.

In many ways, the thematic focus of Isaiah can be categorized as twofold. First, there is a theme of judgment—used to describe the wrongdoings and injustices of humans against humans, and humans against God. And second, there is a theme of hope and salvation—God's promises that in the midst of rebellion, he would still fulfill his covenant promises through a new king, named "Immanuel."

We repeat ash-like gray colors to represent themes of judgment and depict images of torn paper to express Israel's rebellions against God. Elsewhere, we explore the color pink to symbolize messages of hope and salvation. We use the object of a candle to represent Isaiah's foreshadowing of this new king, who will ultimately bring "good news" (Is. 41:27, 61:1).

Ultimately, the themes of judgment and salvation are relevant to us today. Living a beautiful life means a life full of imperfection—there are days where we are far from God's intent for us, and we too need his justice to move towards a better path. Other days seem full of salvation and hope when we experience Immanuel and fully grasp the meaning of "God is with us."

Art is a vessel that helps us ask deeper questions and see things anew. We hope that as you read this Book of Isaiah, it will bring you to ask questions that help you explore what it means for God to be *with* you, and with the world around you. Amen.

BOOK OF

ISAIAH

1

¹ These are the visions that Isaiah son of Amoz saw concerning Judah and Jerusalem. He saw these visions during the years when Uzziah, Jotham, Ahaz, and Hezekiah were kings of Judah.

A MESSAGE FOR REBELLIOUS JUDAH

² Listen, O heavens! Pay attention, earth!
This is what the Lord says: "The children I raised
and cared for have rebelled against me.
³ Even an ox knows its owner, and a donkey
recognizes its master's care
—but Israel doesn't know its master.
My people don't recognize my care for them."
⁴ Oh, what a sinful nation they are—
loaded down with a burden of guilt.
They are evil people,
corrupt children who have rejected the Lord.
They have despised the Holy One of Israel and
turned their backs on him.
⁵ Why do you continue to invite punishment?
Must you rebel forever?
Your head is injured, and your heart is sick.
⁶ You are battered from head to foot—
covered with bruises, welts, and infected wounds—
without any soothing ointments or bandages.
⁷ Your country lies in ruins,
and your towns are burned.
Foreigners plunder your fields before your eyes
and destroy everything they see.
⁸ Beautiful Jerusalem stands abandoned like a
watchman's shelter in a vineyard,
like a lean-to in a cucumber field after the harvest,
like a helpless city under siege.
⁹ If the Lord of Heaven's Armies
had not spared a few of us,
we would have been wiped out like Sodom, destroyed like Gomorrah.
¹⁰ Listen to the Lord, you leaders of "Sodom."
Listen to the law of our God, people of "Gomorrah."
¹¹ "What makes you think I want
all your sacrifices?" says the Lord.
"I am sick of your burnt offerings of rams and
the fat of fattened cattle. I get no pleasure from
the blood of bulls and lambs and goats.
¹² When you come to worship me,
who asked you to parade through my courts

with all your ceremony?

¹³ Stop bringing me your meaningless gifts;
the incense of your offerings disgusts me!
As for your celebrations of the new moon and
the Sabbath and your special days for fasting—
they are all sinful and false.
I want no more of your pious meetings.

¹⁴ I hate your new moon celebrations
and your annual festivals.
They are a burden to me. I cannot stand them!

¹⁵ When you lift up your hands
in prayer, I will not look.
Though you offer many prayers, I will not listen,
for your hands are covered with
the blood of innocent victims.

¹⁶ Wash yourselves and be clean!
Get your sins out of my sight.
Give up your evil ways.

¹⁷ Learn to do good. Seek justice.
Help the oppressed.
Defend the cause of orphans.
Fight for the rights of widows.

¹⁸ "Come now, let's settle this," says the Lord.

"Though your sins are like scarlet, I will make
them as white as snow. Though they are red like
crimson, I will make them as white as wool.

¹⁹ If you will only obey me,
you will have plenty to eat.

²⁰ But if you turn away and refuse to listen,
you will be devoured by the sword of your enemies.
I, the Lord, have spoken!"

UNFAITHFUL JERUSALEM

²¹ See how Jerusalem, once so faithful,
has become a prostitute.
Once the home of justice and righteousness,
she is now filled with murderers.

²² Once like pure silver,
you have become like worthless slag.
Once so pure,
you are now like watered-down wine.

²³ Your leaders are rebels,
the companions of thieves.
All of them love bribes and demand payoffs,
but they refuse to defend the cause of orphans
or fight for the rights of widows.

²⁴ Therefore, the Lord, the Lord of Heaven's Armies,
the Mighty One of Israel, says,
"I will take revenge on my enemies
and pay back my foes!
²⁵ I will raise my fist against you.
I will melt you down and skim off your slag.
I will remove all your impurities.
²⁶ Then I will give you good judges again
and wise counselors like you used to have.
Then Jerusalem will again be called
the Home of Justice and the Faithful City."
²⁷ Zion will be restored by justice;
those who repent will be revived by righteousness.
²⁸ But rebels and sinners will be completely destroyed,
and those who desert the Lord will be consumed.
²⁹ You will be ashamed of your idol worship
in groves of sacred oaks.
You will blush because you worshiped
in gardens dedicated to idols.
³⁰ You will be like a great tree with withered leaves,
like a garden without water.
³¹ The strongest among you will disappear like straw;
their evil deeds will be the spark that sets it on fire.
They and their evil works will burn up together,
and no one will be able to put out the fire.

2

THE LORD'S FUTURE REIGN

¹ This is a vision that Isaiah son of Amoz
saw concerning Judah and Jerusalem:

² In the last days, the mountain of the Lord's house
will be the highest of all—
the most important place on earth.
It will be raised above the other hills,
and people from all over the world will stream there to worship.

³ People from many nations will come and say,
"Come, let us go up to the mountain of the Lord,
to the house of Jacob's God.
There he will teach us his ways,
and we will walk in his paths."
For the Lord's teaching will go out from Zion;
his word will go out from Jerusalem.

⁴ The Lord will mediate between nations
and will settle international disputes.
They will hammer their swords into plowshares
and their spears into pruning hooks.
Nation will no longer fight against nation,
nor train for war anymore.

A WARNING OF JUDGMENT

⁵ Come, descendants of Jacob,
let us walk in the light of the Lord!

⁶ For the Lord has rejected his people,
the descendants of Jacob,
because they have filled their land
with practices from the East
and with sorcerers, as the Philistines do.
They have made alliances with pagans.

⁷ Israel is full of silver and gold;
there is no end to its treasures.
Their land is full of warhorses;
there is no end to its chariots.

⁸ Their land is full of idols;
the people worship things they have made
with their own hands.

⁹ So now they will be humbled,
and all will be brought low—
do not forgive them.

¹⁰ Crawl into caves in the rocks.
Hide in the dust
from the terror of the Lord
and the glory of his majesty.

¹¹ Human pride will be brought down,
and human arrogance will be humbled.
Only the Lord will be exalted
on that day of judgment.

¹² For the Lord of Heaven's Armies
has a day of reckoning.
He will punish the proud and mighty
and bring down everything that is exalted.

¹³ He will cut down the tall cedars of Lebanon
and all the mighty oaks of Bashan.

¹⁴ He will level all the high mountains
and all the lofty hills.

¹⁵ He will break down every high tower
and every fortified wall.

¹⁶ He will destroy all the great trading ships
and every magnificent vessel.

¹⁷ Human pride will be humbled,
and human arrogance will be brought down.
Only the Lord will be exalted
on that day of judgment.

¹⁸ Idols will completely disappear.

¹⁹ When the Lord rises to shake the earth,
his enemies will crawl into holes in the ground.
They will hide in caves in the rocks
from the terror of the Lord
and the glory of his majesty.

²⁰ On that day of judgment they will abandon the
gold and silver idols
they made for themselves to worship.
They will leave their gods
to the rodents and bats,

²¹ while they crawl away into caverns
and hide among the jagged rocks in the cliffs.
They will try to escape the terror of the Lord
and the glory of his majesty
as he rises to shake the earth.

²² Don't put your trust in mere humans.
They are as frail as breath.
What good are they?

3

JUDGMENT AGAINST JUDAH

¹ The Lord, the Lord of Heaven's Armies,
   will take away from Jerusalem and Judah
   everything they depend on:
   every bit of bread
   and every drop of water,
² all their heroes and soldiers,
   judges and prophets,
   fortune-tellers and elders,
³ army officers and high officials,
   advisers, skilled sorcerers, and astrologers.
⁴ I will make boys their leaders,
   and toddlers their rulers.
⁵ People will oppress each other—
   man against man, neighbor against neighbor.
   Young people will insult their elders,
   and vulgar people will sneer at the honorable.
⁶ In those days a man will say to his brother,
   "Since you have a coat, you be our leader!
   Take charge of this heap of ruins!"
⁷ But he will reply,
   "No! I can't help.
   I don't have any extra food or clothes.
   Don't put me in charge!"
⁸ For Jerusalem will stumble,
   and Judah will fall,
   because they speak out against the Lord

and refuse to obey him.
   They provoke him to his face.
⁹ The very look on their faces gives them away.
   They display their sin like the people of Sodom
   and don't even try to hide it.
   They are doomed!
   They have brought destruction upon themselves.
¹⁰ Tell the godly that all will be well for them.
   They will enjoy the rich reward
   they have earned!
¹¹ But the wicked are doomed,
   for they will get exactly what they deserve.
¹² Childish leaders oppress my people,
   and women rule over them.
   O my people, your leaders mislead you;
   they send you down the wrong road.
¹³ The Lord takes his place in court
   and presents his case against his people.
¹⁴ The Lord comes forward
   to pronounce judgment
   on the elders and rulers of his people:
   "You have ruined Israel, my vineyard.
   Your houses are filled with things stolen
   from the poor.
¹⁵ How dare you crush my people,
   grinding the faces of the poor into the dust?"
   demands the Lord, the Lord of Heaven's Armies.

A WARNING TO JERUSALEM

16 The Lord says, "Beautiful Zion is haughty:
craning her elegant neck,
flirting with her eyes,
walking with dainty steps,
tinkling her ankle bracelets.

17 So the Lord will send scabs on her head;
the Lord will make beautiful Zion bald."

18 On that day of judgment
the Lord will strip away everything
that makes her beautiful:
ornaments, headbands, crescent necklaces,

19 earrings, bracelets, and veils;

20 scarves, ankle bracelets, sashes,
perfumes, and charms;

²¹ rings, jewels,

²² party clothes, gowns, capes, and purses;

²³ mirrors, fine linen garments,
   head ornaments, and shawls.

²⁴ Instead of smelling of sweet perfume, she will stink.
   She will wear a rope for a sash,
   and her elegant hair will fall out.
   She will wear rough burlap instead of rich robes.
   Shame will replace her beauty.

²⁵ The men of the city will be killed with the sword,
   and her warriors will die in battle.

²⁶ The gates of Zion will weep and mourn.
   The city will be like a ravaged woman,
   huddled on the ground.

4

¹ In that day so few men will be left that seven women will fight for each man, saying, "Let us all marry you! We will provide our own food and clothing. Only let us take your name so we won't be mocked as old maids."

A PROMISE OF RESTORATION

² But in that day, the branch of the Lord
will be beautiful and glorious;
the fruit of the land will be the pride and glory
of all who survive in Israel.
³ All who remain in Zion
will be a holy people—
those who survive the destruction of Jerusalem
and are recorded among the living.
⁴ The Lord will wash the filth from beautiful Zion
and cleanse Jerusalem of its bloodstains
with the hot breath of fiery judgment.
⁵ Then the Lord will provide shade for Mount Zion
and all who assemble there.
He will provide a canopy of cloud during the day
and smoke and flaming fire at night,
covering the glorious land.
⁶ It will be a shelter from daytime heat
and a hiding place from storms and rain.

5

A SONG ABOUT THE LORD'S VINEYARD

¹ Now I will sing for the one I love
a song about his vineyard:
My beloved had a vineyard
on a rich and fertile hill.

² He plowed the land, cleared its stones,
and planted it with the best vines.
In the middle he built a watchtower
and carved a winepress in the nearby rocks.
Then he waited for a harvest of sweet grapes,
but the grapes that grew were bitter.

³ Now, you people of Jerusalem and Judah,
you judge between me and my vineyard.

⁴ What more could I have done for my vineyard
that I have not already done?
When I expected sweet grapes,
why did my vineyard give me bitter grapes?

⁵ Now let me tell you what I will do to my vineyard:
I will tear down its hedges
and let it be destroyed.
I will break down its walls
and let the animals trample it.

⁶ I will make it a wild place where the vines
are not pruned and the ground is not hoed,
a place overgrown with briers and thorns.
I will command the clouds
to drop no rain on it.

⁷ The nation of Israel is the vineyard of
the Lord of Heaven's Armies.

The people of Judah are his pleasant garden.
He expected a crop of justice,
but instead he found oppression.
He expected to find righteousness,
but instead he heard cries of violence.

JUDAH'S GUILT AND JUDGMENT

⁸ What sorrow for you who buy up house
after house and field after field,
until everyone is evicted
and you live alone in the land.

⁹ But I have heard the Lord of Heaven's Armies
swear a solemn oath:
"Many houses will stand deserted;
even beautiful mansions will be empty.

¹⁰ Ten acres of vineyard will
not produce even six gallons of wine.
Ten baskets of seed will yield
only one basket of grain."

¹¹ What sorrow for those
who get up early in the morning
looking for a drink of alcohol
and spend long evenings drinking wine
to make themselves flaming drunk.

¹² They furnish wine and lovely music
at their grand parties—
lyre and harp, tambourine and flute—
but they never think about the Lord
or notice what he is doing.

¹³ So my people will go into exile far away
because they do not know me.
Those who are great and honored will starve,
and the common people will die of thirst.

¹⁴ The grave is licking its lips in anticipation,
opening its mouth wide.
The great and the lowly and
all the drunken mob will be swallowed up.

¹⁵ Humanity will be destroyed,
and people brought down;
even the arrogant will lower
their eyes in humiliation.

¹⁶ But the Lord of Heaven's Armies
will be exalted by his justice.
The holiness of God will be
displayed by his righteousness.

¹⁷ In that day lambs will find good pastures,
and fattened sheep and young goats
will feed among the ruins.

¹⁸ What sorrow for those who drag their sins
behind them with ropes made of lies,
who drag wickedness behind them like a cart!

¹⁹ They even mock God and say,
"Hurry up and do something!
We want to see what you can do.
Let the Holy One of Israel carry out his plan,
for we want to know what it is."

²⁰ What sorrow for those who say
that evil is good and good is evil,
that dark is light and light is dark,
that bitter is sweet and sweet is bitter.

²¹ What sorrow for those who are wise
in their own eyes and think themselves so clever.

²² What sorrow for those
who are heroes at drinking wine
and boast about all the alcohol they can hold.

²³ They take bribes to let the wicked go free,
and they punish the innocent.

²⁴ Therefore, just as fire licks up stubble
and dry grass shrivels in the flame,
so their roots will rot and their flowers wither.
For they have rejected the law of
the Lord of Heaven's Armies;
they have despised the word
of the Holy One of Israel.

²⁵ That is why the Lord's anger
burns against his people,
and why he has raised his fist to crush them.
The mountains tremble,
and the corpses of his people litter
the streets like garbage.
But even then the Lord's anger is not satisfied.
His fist is still poised to strike!

²⁶ He will send a signal to distant nations far away
and whistle to those at the ends of the earth.
They will come racing toward Jerusalem.

²⁷ They will not get tired or stumble.
They will not stop for rest or sleep.
Not a belt will be loose,
not a sandal strap broken.

²⁸ Their arrows will be sharp
and their bows ready for battle.
Sparks will fly from their horses' hooves,
and the wheels of their
chariots will spin like a whirlwind.

²⁹ They will roar like lions,
like the strongest of lions.
Growling, they will pounce on their victims
and carry them off,
and no one will be there to rescue them.

³⁰ They will roar over their victims on
that day of destruction
like the roaring of the sea.
If someone looks across the land,
only darkness and distress will be seen;
even the light will be darkened by clouds.

6

ISAIAH'S CLEANSING AND CALL

¹ It was in the year King Uzziah died that I saw the Lord. He was sitting on a lofty throne, and the train of his robe filled the Temple. ² Attending him were mighty seraphim, each having six wings. With two wings they covered their faces, with two they covered their feet, and with two they flew. ³ They were calling out to each other,

"Holy, holy, holy is the Lord of Heaven's Armies!
The whole earth is filled with his glory!"

⁴ Their voices shook the Temple to its foundations, and the entire building was filled with smoke. ⁵ Then I said, "It's all over! I am doomed, for I am a sinful man. I have filthy lips, and I live among a people with filthy lips. Yet I have seen the King, the Lord of Heaven's Armies." ⁶ Then one of the seraphim flew to me with a burning coal he had taken from the altar with a pair of tongs. ⁷ He touched my lips with it and said, "See, this coal has touched your lips. Now your guilt is removed, and your sins are forgiven." ⁸ Then I heard the Lord asking, "Whom should I send as a messenger to this people? Who will go for us?"

I said, "Here I am. Send me." ⁹ And he said, "Yes, go, and say to this people,

'Listen carefully, but do not understand.
Watch closely, but learn nothing.'
¹⁰ Harden the hearts of these people.
Plug their ears and shut their eyes.
That way, they will not see with their eyes,
nor hear with their ears,
nor understand with their hearts
and turn to me for healing."

¹¹ Then I said, "Lord, how long will this go on?" And he replied,

"Until their towns are empty,
their houses are deserted,
and the whole country is a wasteland;
¹² until the Lord has sent everyone away,
and the entire land of Israel lies deserted.
¹³ If even a tenth—a remnant—survive,
it will be invaded again and burned.
But as a terebinth or oak tree leaves a stump when
it is cut down, so Israel's stump
will be a holy seed."

7

A MESSAGE FOR AHAZ

¹ When Ahaz, son of Jotham and grandson of Uzziah, was king of Judah, King Rezin of Syria and Pekah son of Remaliah, the king of Israel, set out to attack Jerusalem. However, they were unable to carry out their plan. ² The news had come to the royal court of Judah: "Syria is allied with Israel against us!" So the hearts of the king and his people trembled with fear, like trees shaking in a storm. ³ Then the Lord said to Isaiah, "Take your son Shear-jashub and go out to meet King Ahaz. You will find him at the end of the aqueduct that feeds water into the upper pool, near the road leading to the field where cloth is washed. ⁴ Tell him to stop worrying. Tell him he doesn't need to fear the fierce anger of those two burned-out embers, King Rezin of Syria and Pekah son of Remaliah. ⁵ Yes, the kings of Syria and Israel are plotting against him, saying, ⁶ 'We will attack Judah and capture it for ourselves. Then we will install the son of Tabeel as Judah's king.' ⁷ But this is what the Sovereign Lord says:

"This invasion will never happen;
it will never take place;
⁸ for Syria is no stronger than its capital, Damascus,
and Damascus is no stronger than its king, Rezin.
As for Israel, within sixty-five years
it will be crushed and completely destroyed.
⁹ Israel is no stronger than its capital, Samaria,
and Samaria is no stronger than its king, Pekah son of Remaliah.
Unless your faith is firm,
I cannot make you stand firm."

THE SIGN OF IMMANUEL

[10] Later, the Lord sent this message to King Ahaz: [11] "Ask the Lord your God for a sign of confirmation, Ahaz. Make it as difficult as you want—as high as heaven or as deep as the place of the dead." [12] But the king refused. "No," he said, "I will not test the Lord like that." [13] Then Isaiah said, "Listen well, you royal family of David! Isn't it enough to exhaust human patience? Must you exhaust the patience of my God as well? [14] All right then, the Lord himself will give you the sign. Look! The virgin will conceive a child! She will give birth to a son and will call him Immanuel (which means 'God is with us'). [15] By the time this child is old enough to choose what is right and reject what is wrong, he will be eating yogurt and honey. [16] For before the child is that old, the lands of the two kings you fear so much will both be deserted. [17] "Then the Lord will bring things on you, your nation, and your family unlike anything since Israel broke away from Judah. He will bring the king of Assyria upon you!" [18] In that day the Lord will whistle for the army of southern Egypt and for the army of Assyria. They will swarm around you like flies and bees. [19] They will come in vast hordes and settle in the fertile areas and also in the desolate valleys, caves, and thorny places. [20] In that day the Lord will hire a "razor" from beyond the Euphrates River—the king of Assyria—and use it to shave off everything: your land, your crops, and your people. [21] In that day a farmer will be fortunate to have a cow and two sheep or goats left. [22] Nevertheless, there will be enough milk for everyone because so few people will be left in the land. They will eat their fill of yogurt and honey. [23] In that day the lush vineyards, now worth 1,000 pieces of silver, will become patches of briers and thorns. [24] The entire land will become a vast expanse of briers and thorns, a hunting ground overrun by wildlife. [25] No one will go to the fertile hillsides where the gardens once grew, for briers and thorns will cover them. Cattle, sheep, and goats will graze there.

THE COMING ASSYRIAN INVASION

¹ Then the Lord said to me, "Make a large signboard and clearly write this name on it: Maher-shalal-hash-baz." ² I asked Uriah the priest and Zechariah son of Jeberekiah, both known as honest men, to witness my doing this. ³ Then I slept with my wife, and she became pregnant and gave birth to a son. And the Lord said, "Call him Maher-shalal-hash-baz. ⁴ For before this child is old enough to say 'Papa' or 'Mama,' the king of Assyria will carry away both the abundance of Damascus and the riches of Samaria." ⁵ Then the Lord spoke to me again and said, ⁶ "My care for the people of Judah is like the gently flowing waters of Shiloah, but they have rejected it. They are rejoicing over what will happen to King Rezin and King Pekah. ⁷ Therefore, the Lord will overwhelm them with a mighty flood from the Euphrates River—the king of Assyria and all his glory. This flood will overflow all its channels ⁸ and sweep into Judah until it is chin deep. It will spread its wings, submerging your land from one end to the other, O Immanuel.

⁹ "Huddle together, you nations, and be terrified.
　Listen, all you distant lands.
　Prepare for battle, but you will be crushed!
　Yes, prepare for battle, but you will be crushed!
¹⁰ Call your councils of war,
　but they will be worthless.
　Develop your strategies,
　but they will not succeed.
　For God is with us!"

8

A CALL TO TRUST THE LORD

[11] The Lord has given me a strong warning not to think like everyone else does. He said,

[12] "Don't call everything a conspiracy, like they do,
  and don't live in dread of what frightens them.
[13] Make the Lord of Heaven's Armies holy in your life.
  He is the one you should fear.
  He is the one who should make you tremble.
[14] He will keep you safe. But to Israel and Judah
  he will be a stone that makes people stumble,
  a rock that makes them fall.
  And for the people of Jerusalem he will be a trap and a snare.
[15] Many will stumble and fall, never to rise again.
  They will be snared and captured."
[16] Preserve the teaching of God;
  entrust his instructions to those who follow me.
[17] I will wait for the Lord,
  who has turned away from the descendants of Jacob.
  I will put my hope in him.

[18] I and the children the Lord has given me serve as signs and warnings to Israel from the Lord of Heaven's Armies who dwells in his Temple on Mount Zion. [19] Someone may say to you, "Let's ask the mediums and those who consult the spirits of the dead. With their whisperings and mutterings, they will tell us what to do." But shouldn't people ask God for guidance? Should the living seek guidance from the dead? [20] Look to God's instructions and teachings! People who contradict his word are completely in the dark. [21] They will go from one place to another, weary and hungry. And because they are hungry, they will rage and curse their king and their God. They will look up to heaven [22] and down at the earth, but wherever they look, there will be trouble and anguish and dark despair. They will be thrown out into the darkness.

9

HOPE IN THE MESSIAH

[1] Nevertheless, that time of darkness and despair will not go on forever. The land of Zebulun and Naphtali will be humbled, but there will be a time in the future when Galilee of the Gentiles, which lies along the road that runs between the Jordan and the sea, will be filled with glory.

[2] The people who walk in darkness
will see a great light.
For those who live in a land of
deep darkness, a light will shine.
[3] You will enlarge the nation of Israel,
and its people will rejoice.
They will rejoice before you
as people rejoice at the harvest
and like warriors dividing the plunder.
[4] For you will break the yoke of their slavery
and lift the heavy burden from their shoulders.
You will break the oppressor's rod,

just as you did when you destroyed
the army of Midian.
[5] The boots of the warrior
and the uniforms bloodstained by war
will all be burned.
They will be fuel for the fire.
[6] For a child is born to us,
a son is given to us.
The government will rest on his shoulders.
And he will be called:
Wonderful Counselor, Mighty God,
Everlasting Father, Prince of Peace.
[7] His government and its peace
will never end.
He will rule with fairness and justice
from the throne of his ancestor David
for all eternity.
The passionate commitment of the Lord of
Heaven's Armies will make this happen!

THE LORD'S ANGER AGAINST ISRAEL

8 The Lord has spoken out against Jacob;
his judgment has fallen upon Israel.

9 And the people of Israel and Samaria,
who spoke with such pride and arrogance,
will soon know it.

10 They said, "We will replace the broken bricks
of our ruins with finished stone,
and replant the felled
sycamore-fig trees with cedars."

11 But the Lord will bring Rezin's
enemies against Israel
and stir up all their foes.

12 The Syrians from the east and
the Philistines from the west
will bare their fangs and devour Israel.
But even then the Lord's anger will not be satisfied.
His fist is still poised to strike.

13 For after all this punishment,
the people will still not repent.
They will not seek the Lord of Heaven's Armies.

14 Therefore, in a single day the Lord will destroy
both the head and the tail,
the noble palm branch and the lowly reed.

15 The leaders of Israel are the head,
and the lying prophets are the tail.

16 For the leaders of the people have misled them.
They have led them

down the path of destruction.

17 That is why the Lord takes
no pleasure in the young men
and shows no mercy
even to the widows and orphans.
For they are all wicked hypocrites,
and they all speak foolishness.
But even then the Lord's anger will not be satisfied.
His fist is still poised to strike.

18 This wickedness is like a brushfire.
It burns not only briers and thorns
but also sets the forests ablaze.
Its burning sends up clouds of smoke.

19 The land will be blackened
by the fury of the Lord of Heaven's Armies.
The people will be fuel for the fire,
and no one will spare even his own brother.

20 They will attack their neighbor on the right
but will still be hungry.
They will devour their neighbor on the left
but will not be satisfied.
In the end they will even eat their own children.

21 Manasseh will feed on Ephraim,
Ephraim will feed on Manasseh,
and both will devour Judah.
But even then the Lord's anger
will not be satisfied.
His fist is still poised to strike.

10

¹ What sorrow awaits the unjust judges
and those who issue unfair laws.
² They deprive the poor of justice and
deny the rights of the needy among my people.
They prey on widows
and take advantage of orphans.
³ What will you do when I punish you,
when I send disaster upon you from a distant land?
To whom will you turn for help?
Where will your treasures be safe?
⁴ You will stumble along as prisoners or lie
among the dead. But even then the Lord's anger
will not be satisfied. His fist is still poised to strike.

JUDGMENT AGAINST ASSYRIA

⁵ "What sorrow awaits Assyria, the rod of my anger.
I use it as a club to express my anger.

⁶ I am sending Assyria against a godless nation,
against a people with whom I am angry.
Assyria will plunder them,
trampling them like dirt beneath its feet.
⁷ But the king of Assyria will
not understand that he is my tool;
his mind does not work that way.
His plan is simply to destroy,
to cut down nation after nation.
⁸ He will say,
'Each of my princes will soon be a king.
⁹ We destroyed Calno just as we did Carchemish.
Hamath fell before us as Arpad did.
And we destroyed Samaria just as we did Damascus.
¹⁰ Yes, we have finished off
many a kingdom whose gods
were greater than those in Jerusalem and Samaria.

¹¹ So we will defeat Jerusalem and her gods,
just as we destroyed Samaria with hers.'"

¹² After the Lord has used the king of Assyria to accomplish his purposes on Mount Zion and in Jerusalem, he will turn against the king of Assyria and punish him—for he is proud and arrogant. ¹³ He boasts,

"By my own powerful arm I have done this.
With my own shrewd wisdom I planned it.
I have broken down the defenses of nations
and carried off their treasures.
I have knocked down their kings like a bull.
¹⁴ I have robbed their nests of riches and
gathered up kingdoms as a farmer gathers eggs.
No one can even flap a wing against me

or utter a peep of protest."

¹⁵ But can the ax boast greater power than the person who uses it? Is the saw greater than the person who saws? Can a rod strike unless a hand moves it? Can a wooden cane walk by itself?

¹⁶ Therefore, the Lord, the Lord of Heaven's Armies, will send a plague among Assyria's proud troops, and a flaming fire will consume its glory.

¹⁷ The Lord, the Light of Israel, will be a fire;
the Holy One will be a flame.
He will devour the thorns and briers with fire,
burning up the enemy in a single night.

¹⁸ The Lord will consume Assyria's glory
like a fire consumes a forest in a fruitful land;
it will waste away like sick people in a plague.

¹⁹ Of all that glorious forest, only a few trees will survive—so few that a child could count them!

HOPE FOR THE LORD'S PEOPLE

20 In that day the remnant left in Israel,
the survivors in the house of Jacob,
will no longer depend on allies
who seek to destroy them.
But they will faithfully trust the Lord,
the Holy One of Israel.

21 A remnant will return;
yes, the remnant of Jacob will return
to the Mighty God.

22 But though the people of Israel are
as numerous as the sand of the seashore,
only a remnant of them will return.
The Lord has rightly decided to destroy his people.

23 Yes, the Lord, the Lord of Heaven's Armies,
has already decided to destroy the entire land.

24 So this is what the Lord, the Lord of Heaven's Armies, says: "O my people in Zion, do not be afraid of the Assyrians when they oppress you with rod and club as the Egyptians did long ago. 25 In a little while my anger against you will end, and then my anger will rise up to destroy them." 26 The Lord of Heaven's Armies will lash them with his whip, as he did when Gideon triumphed over the Midianites at the rock of Oreb, or when the Lord's staff was raised to drown the Egyptian army in the sea.

27 In that day the Lord will end
the bondage of his people.
He will break the yoke of slavery
and lift it from their shoulders.

28 Look, the Assyrians are now at Aiath.
They are passing through Migron
and are storing their equipment at Micmash.

29 They are crossing the pass and are camping at Geba.
Fear strikes the town of Ramah.
All the people of Gibeah, the hometown of Saul,
are running for their lives.

30 Scream in terror,
you people of Gallim!
Shout out a warning to Laishah.
Oh, poor Anathoth!

31 There go the people of Madmenah, all fleeing.
The citizens of Gebim are trying to hide.

32 The enemy stops at Nob for the rest of that day.
He shakes his fist at beautiful Mount Zion,
the mountain of Jerusalem.

33 But look! The Lord, the Lord of Heaven's Armies,
will chop down the mighty tree of
Assyria with great power!

34 He will cut down the proud.
That lofty tree will be brought down.
He will cut down the forest trees with an ax.
Lebanon will fall to the Mighty One.

11

A BRANCH FROM DAVID'S LINE

¹ Out of the stump of David's family
will grow a shoot—
yes, a new Branch bearing fruit from the old root.
² And the Spirit of the Lord will rest on him—
the Spirit of wisdom and understanding,
the Spirit of counsel and might,
the Spirit of knowledge and the fear of the Lord.
³ He will delight in obeying the Lord.
He will not judge by appearance
nor make a decision based on hearsay.
⁴ He will give justice to the poor
and make fair decisions for the exploited.
The earth will shake at the force of his word,
and one breath from his mouth
will destroy the wicked.
⁵ He will wear righteousness like a belt
and truth like an undergarment.
⁶ In that day the wolf and the lamb will live together;
the leopard will lie down with the baby goat.
The calf and the yearling will be safe with the lion,
and a little child will lead them all.
⁷ The cow will graze near the bear.
The cub and the calf will lie down together.
The lion will eat hay like a cow.
⁸ The baby will play safely near the hole of a cobra.
Yes, a little child will put its hand in a nest of
deadly snakes without harm.
⁹ Nothing will hurt or destroy
in all my holy mountain,
for as the waters fill the sea,
so the earth will be filled with
people who know the Lord.
¹⁰ In that day the heir to David's throne

will be a banner of salvation to all the world.
The nations will rally to him,
and the land where he lives will be a glorious place.
¹¹ In that day the Lord will reach out his
hand a second time
to bring back the remnant of his people—
those who remain in Assyria and northern Egypt;
in southern Egypt, Ethiopia, and Elam;
in Babylonia, Hamath,
and all the distant coastlands.
¹² He will raise a flag among the nations
and assemble the exiles of Israel.
He will gather the scattered people of Judah
from the ends of the earth.
¹³ Then at last the jealousy between
Israel and Judah will end.
They will not be rivals anymore.
¹⁴ They will join forces to swoop down
on Philistia to the west.
Together they will attack and plunder
the nations to the east.
They will occupy the lands of Edom and Moab,
and Ammon will obey them.
¹⁵ The Lord will make a dry path
through the gulf of the Red Sea.
He will wave his hand over the Euphrates River,
sending a mighty wind
to divide it into seven streams
so it can easily be crossed on foot.
¹⁶ He will make a highway
for the remnant of his people,
the remnant coming from Assyria,
just as he did for Israel long ago
when they returned from Egypt.

12

SONGS OF PRAISE FOR SALVATION

¹ In that day you will sing:
"I will praise you, O Lord!
You were angry with me, but not any more.
Now you comfort me.
² See, God has come to save me.
I will trust in him and not be afraid.
The Lord God is my strength and my song;
he has given me victory."
³ With joy you will drink deeply
from the fountain of salvation!
⁴ In that wonderful day you will sing:
"Thank the Lord! Praise his name!
Tell the nations what he has done.
Let them know how mighty he is!
⁵ Sing to the Lord, for he has done wonderful things.
Make known his praise around the world.
⁶ Let all the people of Jerusalem shout his praise with joy!
For great is the Holy One of Israel who lives among you."

13

A MESSAGE ABOUT BABYLON

¹ Isaiah son of Amoz received this message concerning the destruction of Babylon:

² "Raise a signal flag on a bare hilltop.
Call up an army against Babylon.
Wave your hand to encourage them
as they march into the palaces
of the high and mighty.
³ I, the Lord, have dedicated
these soldiers for this task.
Yes, I have called mighty warriors
to express my anger,
and they will rejoice when I am exalted."
⁴ Hear the noise on the mountains!
Listen, as the vast armies march!
It is the noise and shouting of many nations.
The Lord of Heaven's Armies has
called this army together.
⁵ They come from distant countries,
from beyond the farthest horizons.
They are the Lord's weapons to carry out his anger.
With them he will destroy the whole land.
⁶ Scream in terror, for the day of the Lord has arrived—
the time for the Almighty to destroy.
⁷ Every arm is paralyzed with fear.
Every heart melts,
⁸ and people are terrified.
Pangs of anguish grip them,
like those of a woman in labor.
They look helplessly at one another,
their faces aflame with fear.
⁹ For see, the day of the Lord is coming—
the terrible day of his fury and fierce anger.
The land will be made desolate,
and all the sinners destroyed with it.
¹⁰ The heavens will be black above them;
the stars will give no light.
The sun will be dark when it rises,
and the moon will provide no light.
¹¹ "I, the Lord, will punish the world for its evil
and the wicked for their sin.
I will crush the arrogance of the proud

and humble the pride of the mighty.
¹² I will make people scarcer than gold—
more rare than the fine gold of Ophir.
¹³ For I will shake the heavens.
The earth will move from its place
when the Lord of Heaven's Armies
displays his wrath
in the day of his fierce anger."
¹⁴ Everyone in Babylon will run about
like a hunted gazelle,
like sheep without a shepherd.
They will try to find their own people
and flee to their own land.
¹⁵ Anyone who is captured will be cut down—
run through with a sword.
¹⁶ Their little children will be dashed to
death before their eyes.
Their homes will be sacked,
and their wives will be raped.
¹⁷ "Look, I will stir up the Medes against Babylon.
They cannot be tempted by silver

or bribed with gold.
¹⁸ The attacking armies will shoot down the young
men with arrows.
They will have no mercy on helpless babies
and will show no compassion for children."
¹⁹ Babylon, the most glorious of kingdoms,
the flower of Chaldean pride,
will be devastated like Sodom and Gomorrah
when God destroyed them.
²⁰ Babylon will never be inhabited again.
It will remain empty for generation after generation.
Nomads will refuse to camp there,
and shepherds will not bed down their sheep.
²¹ Desert animals will move into the ruined city,
and the houses will be haunted by howling creatures.
Owls will live among the ruins,
and wild goats will go there to dance.
²² Hyenas will howl in its fortresses,
and jackals will make dens in its luxurious palaces.
Babylon's days are numbered;
its time of destruction will soon arrive.

14

A TAUNT FOR BABYLON'S KING

¹ But the Lord will have mercy on the descendants of Jacob. He will choose Israel as his special people once again. He will bring them back to settle once again in their own land. And people from many different nations will come and join them there and unite with the people of Israel. ² The nations of the world will help the people of Israel to return, and those who come to live in the Lord's land will serve them. Those who captured Israel will themselves be captured, and Israel will rule over its enemies. ³ In that wonderful day when the Lord gives his people rest from sorrow and fear, from slavery and chains, ⁴ you will taunt the king of Babylon. You will say,

> "The mighty man has been destroyed.
> Yes, your insolence is ended.
> ⁵ For the Lord has crushed your wicked power
> and broken your evil rule.
> ⁶ You struck the people with endless blows of rage
> and held the nations in your angry grip
> with unrelenting tyranny.

> ⁷ But finally the earth is at rest and quiet.
> Now it can sing again!
> ⁸ Even the trees of the forest—
> the cypress trees and the cedars of Lebanon—
> sing out this joyous song:
> 'Since you have been cut down,
> no one will come now to cut us down!'
> ⁹ "In the place of the dead there is excitement
> over your arrival.
> The spirits of world leaders and mighty
> kings long dead stand up to see you.
> ¹⁰ With one voice they all cry out,
> 'Now you are as weak as we are!
> ¹¹ Your might and power were buried with you.
> The sound of the harp in your palace has ceased.
> Now maggots are your sheet,
> and worms your blanket.'
> ¹² "How you are fallen from heaven,
> O shining star, son of the morning!
> You have been thrown down to the earth,
> you who destroyed the nations of the world.
> ¹³ For you said to yourself,
> 'I will ascend to heaven and set my

throne above God's stars.

I will preside on the mountain of the gods
far away in the north.

14 I will climb to the highest heavens
and be like the Most High.'

15 Instead, you will be brought down
to the place of the dead,
down to its lowest depths.

16 Everyone there will stare at you and ask,
'Can this be the one who shook the earth
and made the kingdoms of the world tremble?

17 Is this the one who destroyed the world
and made it into a wasteland?
Is this the king who demolished
the world's greatest cities
and had no mercy on his prisoners?'

18 "The kings of the nations lie in stately glory,
each in his own tomb,

19 but you will be thrown out of your grave
like a worthless branch.
Like a corpse trampled underfoot,
you will be dumped into a mass grave
with those killed in battle.
You will descend to the pit.

20 You will not be given a proper burial,
for you have destroyed your nation
and slaughtered your people.
The descendants of such an evil person
will never again receive honor.

21 Kill this man's children!
Let them die because of their father's sins!
They must not rise and conquer the earth,
filling the world with their cities."

22 This is what the Lord of Heaven's Armies says:
"I, myself, have risen against Babylon!
I will destroy its children
and its children's children,"
says the Lord.

23 "I will make Babylon a desolate place of owls,

filled with swamps and marshes.
I will sweep the land with the broom of destruction.
I, the Lord of Heaven's Armies, have spoken!"

A MESSAGE ABOUT ASSYRIA

24 The Lord of Heaven's Armies has sworn this oath:
"It will all happen as I have planned.
It will be as I have decided.

25 I will break the Assyrians when they are in Israel;
I will trample them on my mountains.
My people will no longer be their slaves
nor bow down under their heavy loads.

26 I have a plan for the whole earth,
a hand of judgment upon all the nations.

27 The Lord of Heaven's Armies has spoken—
who can change his plans?
When his hand is raised,
who can stop him?"

A MESSAGE ABOUT PHILISTIA

28 This message came to me the year King Ahaz died:

29 Do not rejoice, you Philistines,
that the rod that struck you is broken—
that the king who attacked you is dead.
For from that snake a more poisonous
snake will be born,
a fiery serpent to destroy you!

30 I will feed the poor in my pasture;
the needy will lie down in peace.
But as for you, I will wipe you out with famine
and destroy the few who remain.

31 Wail at the gates! Weep in the cities!
Melt with fear, you Philistines!
A powerful army comes like smoke from the north.
Each soldier rushes forward eager to fight.

32 What should we tell the Philistine messengers?
Tell them,
"The Lord has built Jerusalem;
its walls will give refuge to his oppressed people."

15

A MESSAGE ABOUT MOAB

¹ This message came to me concerning Moab:

In one night the town of Ar will be leveled,

and the city of Kir will be destroyed.

² Your people will go to their temple in Dibon to mourn.

They will go to their sacred shrines to weep.

They will wail for the fate of Nebo and Medeba,

shaving their heads in sorrow and cutting off their beards.

³ They will wear burlap as they wander the streets.

From every home and public square will come the sound of wailing.

⁴ The people of Heshbon and Elealeh will cry out;

their voices will be heard as far away as Jahaz!

The bravest warriors of Moab will cry out in utter terror.

They will be helpless with fear.

⁵ My heart weeps for Moab.

Its people flee to Zoar and Eglath-shelishiyah.

Weeping, they climb the road to Luhith.

Their cries of distress can be heard all along the road to Horonaim.

⁶ Even the waters of Nimrim are dried up!

The grassy banks are scorched.

The tender plants are gone;

nothing green remains.

⁷ The people grab their possessions

and carry them across the Ravine of Willows.

⁸ A cry of distress echoes through the land of Moab

from one end to the other—

from Eglaim to Beer-elim.

⁹ The stream near Dibon runs red with blood,

but I am still not finished with Dibon!

Lions will hunt down the survivors—

both those who try to escape

and those who remain behind.

16

¹ Send lambs from Sela as tribute
  to the ruler of the land.
  Send them through the desert
  to the mountain of beautiful Zion.
² The women of Moab are left like homeless birds
  at the shallow crossings of the Arnon River.
³ "Help us," they cry.
  "Defend us against our enemies.
  Protect us from their relentless attack.
  Do not betray us now that we have escaped.
⁴ Let our refugees stay among you.
  Hide them from our enemies
  until the terror is past."
  When oppression and destruction have ended
  and enemy raiders have disappeared,
⁵ then God will establish one of
  David's descendants as king.
  He will rule with mercy and truth.
  He will always do what is just
  and be eager to do what is right.
⁶ We have heard about proud Moab—
  about its pride and arrogance and rage.
  But all that boasting has disappeared.
⁷ The entire land of Moab weeps.
  Yes, everyone in Moab mourns
  for the cakes of raisins from Kir-hareseth.
  They are all gone now.
⁸ The farms of Heshbon are abandoned;
  the vineyards at Sibmah are deserted.
  The rulers of the nations
  have broken down Moab—
  that beautiful grapevine.
  Its tendrils spread north as far as the town of Jazer
  and trailed eastward into the wilderness.
  Its shoots reached so far west
  that they crossed over the Dead Sea.
⁹ So now I weep for Jazer and
  the vineyards of Sibmah;
  my tears will flow for Heshbon and Elealeh.
  There are no more shouts of joy
  over your summer fruits and harvest.
¹⁰ Gone now is the gladness,
  gone the joy of harvest.
  There will be no singing in the vineyards,
  no more happy shouts,
  no treading of grapes in the winepresses.
  I have ended all their harvest joys.
¹¹ My heart's cry for Moab is like a lament on a harp.
  I am filled with anguish for Kir-hareseth.
¹² The people of Moab will
  worship at their pagan shrines,
  but it will do them no good.
  They will cry to the gods in their temples,
  but no one will be able to save them.

¹³ The Lord has already said these things about Moab in the past. ¹⁴ But now the Lord says, "Within three years, counting each day, the glory of Moab will be ended. From its great population, only a feeble few will be left alive."

17

A MESSAGE ABOUT DAMASCUS AND ISRAEL

¹ This message came to me concerning Damascus:
"Look, the city of Damascus will disappear!
It will become a heap of ruins.
² The towns of Aroer will be deserted.
Flocks will graze in the streets
and lie down undisturbed,
with no one to chase them away.
³ The fortified towns of Israel will also be destroyed,
and the royal power of Damascus will end.
All that remains of Syria
will share the fate of Israel's departed glory,"
declares the Lord of Heaven's Armies.
⁴ "In that day Israel's glory will grow dim;
its robust body will waste away.
⁵ The whole land will look like a grainfield
after the harvesters have gathered the grain.
It will be desolate,
like the fields in the valley of Rephaim
after the harvest.
⁶ Only a few of its people will be left,
like stray olives left on a tree after the harvest.
Only two or three remain in the highest branches,
four or five scattered here and there on the limbs,"
declares the Lord, the God of Israel.
⁷ Then at last the people will look to their Creator
and turn their eyes to the Holy One of Israel.
⁸ They will no longer look to their idols for help
or worship what their own hands have made.
They will never again
bow down to their Asherah poles
or worship at the pagan shrines they have built.
⁹ Their largest cities will be like a deserted forest,
like the land the Hivites and Amorites abandoned
when the Israelites came here so long ago.
It will be utterly desolate.

[10] Why? Because you have turned

from the God who can save you.

You have forgotten the Rock who can hide you.

So you may plant the finest grapevines

and import the most expensive seedlings.

[11] They may sprout on the day you set them out;

yes, they may blossom on the very morning you plant them,

but you will never pick any grapes from them.

Your only harvest will be a load of grief and unrelieved pain.

[12] Listen! The armies of many nations

roar like the roaring of the sea.

Hear the thunder of the mighty forces

as they rush forward like thundering waves.

[13] But though they thunder like breakers on a beach,

God will silence them, and they will run away.

They will flee like chaff scattered by the wind,

like a tumbleweed whirling before a storm.

[14] In the evening Israel waits in terror,

but by dawn its enemies are dead.

This is the just reward of those who plunder us,

a fitting end for those who destroy us.

18

A MESSAGE ABOUT ETHIOPIA

1 Listen, Ethiopia—land of fluttering sails
that lies at the headwaters of the Nile,
2 that sends ambassadors
in swift boats down the river.
Go, swift messengers!
Take a message to a tall, smooth-skinned people,
who are feared far and wide
for their conquests and destruction,
and whose land is divided by rivers.
3 All you people of the world,
everyone who lives on the earth—
when I raise my battle flag on the mountain, look!
When I blow the ram's horn, listen!
4 For the Lord has told me this:
"I will watch quietly from my dwelling place—
as quietly as the heat rises on a summer day,
or as the morning dew forms during the harvest."

5 Even before you begin your attack,
while your plans are ripening like grapes,
the Lord will cut off your new growth with
pruning shears.
He will snip off and discard
your spreading branches.
6 Your mighty army will be left dead in the fields
for the mountain vultures and wild animals.
The vultures will tear at the corpses all summer.
The wild animals will gnaw at the bones all winter.
7 At that time the Lord of Heaven's Armies
will receive gifts
from this land divided by rivers,
from this tall, smooth-skinned people,
who are feared far and wide for their conquests
and destruction.
They will bring the gifts to Jerusalem,
where the Lord of Heaven's Armies dwells.

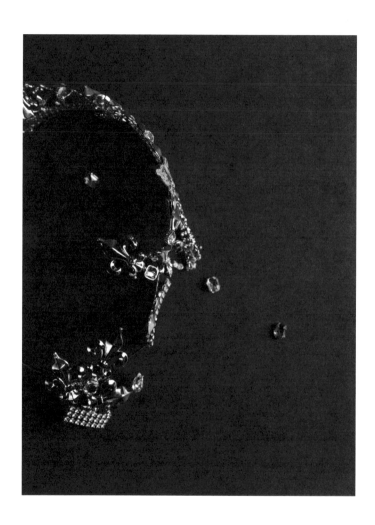

19

A MESSAGE ABOUT EGYPT

1 This message came to me concerning Egypt:
Look! The Lord is advancing against Egypt,
riding on a swift cloud.
The idols of Egypt tremble.
The hearts of the Egyptians melt with fear.
2 "I will make Egyptian fight against Egyptian—
brother against brother,
neighbor against neighbor,
city against city,
province against province.
3 The Egyptians will lose heart,
and I will confuse their plans.
They will plead with their idols for wisdom
and call on spirits, mediums, and those who consult
the spirits of the dead.
4 I will hand Egypt over
to a hard, cruel master.
A fierce king will rule them,"
says the Lord, the Lord of Heaven's Armies.
5 The waters of the Nile will fail to rise
and flood the fields.
The riverbed will be parched and dry.
6 The canals of the Nile will dry up,
and the streams of Egypt will stink
with rotting reeds and rushes.
7 All the greenery along the riverbank
and all the crops along the river
will dry up and blow away.

8 The fishermen will lament for lack of work.
Those who cast hooks into the Nile will groan,
and those who use nets will lose heart.
9 There will be no flax for the harvesters,
no thread for the weavers.
10 They will be in despair,
and all the workers will be sick at heart.
11 What fools are the officials of Zoan!
Their best counsel to the king of Egypt
is stupid and wrong.
Will they still boast to Pharaoh of their wisdom?
Will they dare brag about all their wise ancestors?
12 Where are your wise counselors, Pharaoh?
Let them tell you what God plans,
what the Lord of Heaven's Armies
is going to do to Egypt.
13 The officials of Zoan are fools,
and the officials of Memphis are deluded.
The leaders of the people
have led Egypt astray.
14 The Lord has sent a spirit of foolishness on them,
so all their suggestions are wrong.
They cause Egypt to stagger
like a drunk in his vomit.
15 There is nothing Egypt can do.
All are helpless—
the head and the tail,
the noble palm branch
and the lowly reed.

[16] In that day the Egyptians will be as weak as women. They will cower in fear beneath the upraised fist of the Lord of Heaven's Armies. [17] Just to speak the name of Israel will terrorize them, for the Lord of Heaven's Armies has laid out his plans against them. [18] In that day five of Egypt's cities will follow the Lord of Heaven's Armies. They will even begin to speak Hebrew, the language of Canaan. One of these cities will be Heliopolis, the City of the Sun. [19] In that day there will be an altar to the Lord in the heart of Egypt, and there will be a monument to the Lord at its border. [20] It will be a sign and a witness that the Lord of Heaven's Armies is worshiped in the land of Egypt. When the people cry to the Lord for help against those who oppress them, he will send them a savior who will rescue them. [21] The Lord will make himself known to the Egyptians. Yes, they will know the Lord and will give their sacrifices and offerings to him. They will make a vow to the Lord and will keep it. [22] The Lord will strike Egypt, and then he will bring healing. For the Egyptians will turn to the Lord, and he will listen to their pleas and heal them. [23] In that day Egypt and Assyria will be connected by a highway. The Egyptians and Assyrians will move freely between their lands, and they will both worship God. [24] In that day Israel will be the third, along with Egypt and Assyria, a blessing in the midst of the earth. [25] For the Lord of Heaven's Armies will say, "Blessed be Egypt, my people. Blessed be Assyria, the land I have made. Blessed be Israel, my special possession!"

20

A MESSAGE ABOUT EGYPT AND ETHIOPIA

[1] In the year when King Sargon of Assyria sent his commander in chief to capture the Philistine city of Ashdod, [2] the Lord told Isaiah son of Amoz, "Take off the burlap you have been wearing, and remove your sandals." Isaiah did as he was told and walked around naked and barefoot. [3] Then the Lord said, "My servant Isaiah has been walking around naked and barefoot for the last three years. This is a sign—a symbol of the terrible troubles I will bring upon Egypt and Ethiopia. [4] For the king of Assyria will take away the Egyptians and Ethiopians as prisoners. He will make them walk naked and barefoot, both young and old, their buttocks bared, to the shame of Egypt. [5] Then the Philistines will be thrown into panic, for they counted on the power of Ethiopia and boasted of their allies in Egypt! [6] They will say, 'If this can happen to Egypt, what chance do we have? We were counting on Egypt to protect us from the king of Assyria.'"

21

A MESSAGE ABOUT BABYLON

[1] This message came to me concerning Babylon—
the desert by the sea:

Disaster is roaring down on you from the desert,
like a whirlwind sweeping in from the Negev.
[2] I see a terrifying vision:
I see the betrayer betraying,
the destroyer destroying.
Go ahead, you Elamites and Medes,
attack and lay siege.
I will make an end
to all the groaning Babylon caused.

[3] My stomach aches and burns with pain.
Sharp pangs of anguish are upon me,
like those of a woman in labor.
I grow faint when I hear what God is planning;
I am too afraid to look.
[4] My mind reels and my heart races.
I longed for evening to come,
but now I am terrified of the dark.
[5] Look! They are preparing a great feast.
They are spreading rugs for people to sit on.
Everyone is eating and drinking.
But quick! Grab your shields and prepare for battle.
You are being attacked!

6 Meanwhile, the Lord said to me,
  "Put a watchman on the city wall.
  Let him shout out what he sees.
7 He should look for chariots
  drawn by pairs of horses,
  and for riders on donkeys and camels.
  Let the watchman be fully alert."
8 Then the watchman called out,
  "Day after day I have stood
  on the watchtower, my lord.
  Night after night I have remained at my post.
9 Now at last—look!
  Here comes a man in a chariot
  with a pair of horses!"
  Then the watchman said,
  "Babylon is fallen, fallen!
  All the idols of Babylon
  lie broken on the ground!"
10 O my people, threshed and winnowed,
  I have told you everything the
  Lord of Heaven's Armies has said,
  everything the God of Israel has told me.

A MESSAGE ABOUT EDOM

[11] This message came to me concerning Edom:

Someone from Edom keeps calling to me,

"Watchman, how much longer until morning?

When will the night be over?"

[12] The watchman replies,

"Morning is coming, but night will soon return.

If you wish to ask again, then come back and ask."

A MESSAGE ABOUT ARABIA

[13] This message came to me concerning Arabia:

O caravans from Dedan,

hide in the deserts of Arabia.

[14] O people of Tema,

bring water to these thirsty people,

food to these weary refugees.

[15] They have fled from the sword,

from the drawn sword,

from the bent bow

and the terrors of battle.

[16] The Lord said to me, "Within a year, counting each day, all the glory of Kedar will come to an end. [17] Only a few of its courageous archers will survive. I, the Lord, the God of Israel, have spoken!"

22

A MESSAGE ABOUT JERUSALEM

¹ This message came to me concerning Jerusalem—
the Valley of Vision:
What is happening?
Why is everyone running to the rooftops?
² The whole city is in a terrible uproar.
What do I see in this reveling city?
Bodies are lying everywhere,
killed not in battle but
by famine and disease.
³ All your leaders have fled.
They surrendered without resistance.
The people tried to slip away,
but they were captured, too.
⁴ That's why I said, "Leave me alone to weep;
do not try to comfort me.
Let me cry for my people
as I watch them being destroyed."
⁵ Oh, what a day of crushing defeat!
What a day of confusion and terror
brought by the Lord, the Lord of Heaven's Armies,
upon the Valley of Vision!
The walls of Jerusalem have been broken,
and cries of death echo from the mountainsides.
⁶ Elamites are the archers,
with their chariots and charioteers.
The men of Kir hold up the shields.
⁷ Chariots fill your beautiful valleys,
and charioteers storm your gates.
⁸ Judah's defenses have been stripped away.
You run to the armory for your weapons.
⁹ You inspect the breaks in the walls of Jerusalem.
You store up water in the lower pool.
¹⁰ You survey the houses and tear some down
for stone to strengthen the walls.
¹¹ Between the city walls, you build a reservoir
for water from the old pool.
But you never ask for help from
the One who did all this.
You never considered the
One who planned this long ago.
¹² At that time the Lord, the Lord of Heaven's Armies,
called you to weep and mourn.
He told you to shave your
heads in sorrow for your sins
and to wear clothes of burlap to show your remorse.
¹³ But instead, you dance and play;
you slaughter cattle and kill sheep.
You feast on meat and drink wine.
You say, "Let's feast and drink,
for tomorrow we die!"

¹⁴ The Lord of Heaven's Armies has revealed this to me: "Till the day you die, you will never be forgiven for this sin." That is the judgment of the Lord, the Lord of Heaven's Armies.

A MESSAGE FOR SHEBNA

¹⁵ This is what the Lord, the Lord of Heaven's Armies, said to me: "Confront Shebna, the palace administrator, and give him this message:

¹⁶ "Who do you think you are,
   and what are you doing here,
   building a beautiful tomb for yourself—
   a monument high up in the rock?
¹⁷ For the Lord is about to hurl you away, mighty man.
   He is going to grab you,
¹⁸ crumple you into a ball,
   and toss you away into a distant, barren land.
   There you will die,
   and your glorious chariots will be broken and useless.
   You are a disgrace to your master!

¹⁹ "Yes, I will drive you out of office," says the Lord. "I will pull you down from your high position. ²⁰ And then I will call my servant Eliakim son of Hilkiah to replace you. ²¹ I will dress him in your royal robes and will give him your title and your authority. And he will be a father to the people of Jerusalem and Judah. ²² I will give him the key to the house of David—the highest position in the royal court. When he opens doors, no one will be able to close them; when he closes doors, no one will be able to open them. ²³ He will bring honor to his family name, for I will drive him firmly in place like a nail in the wall. ²⁴ They will give him great responsibility, and he will bring honor to even the lowliest members of his family." ²⁵ But the Lord of Heaven's Armies also says: "The time will come when I will pull out the nail that seemed so firm. It will come out and fall to the ground. Everything it supports will fall with it. I, the Lord, have spoken!"

23

A MESSAGE ABOUT TYRE

¹ This message came to me concerning Tyre:
Wail, you trading ships of Tarshish,
for the harbor and houses of Tyre are gone!
The rumors you heard in Cyprus
are all true.

² Mourn in silence, you people of the coast
 and you merchants of Sidon.
Your traders crossed the sea,

³ sailing over deep waters.
They brought you grain from Egypt
and harvests from along the Nile.
You were the marketplace of the world.

⁴ But now you are put to shame, city of Sidon,
for Tyre, the fortress of the sea, says,
"Now I am childless;
I have no sons or daughters."

⁵ When Egypt hears the news about Tyre,
there will be great sorrow.

⁶ Send word now to Tarshish!
Wail, you people who live in distant lands!

⁷ Is this silent ruin all that is left
of your once joyous city?
What a long history was yours!
Think of all the colonists
you sent to distant places.

⁸ Who has brought this disaster on Tyre,
that great creator of kingdoms?
Her traders were all princes,
her merchants were nobles.

⁹ The Lord of Heaven's Armies has done it
to destroy your pride
and bring low all earth's nobility.

¹⁰ Come, people of Tarshish,
sweep over the land like the flooding Nile,
for Tyre is defenseless.

¹¹ The Lord held out his hand over the sea
and shook the kingdoms of the earth.
He has spoken out against Phoenicia,
ordering that her fortresses be destroyed.

¹² He says, "Never again will you rejoice,
O daughter of Sidon, for you have been crushed.
Even if you flee to Cyprus,
you will find no rest."

¹³ Look at the land of Babylonia—
  the people of that land are gone!
  The Assyrians have handed Babylon over
  to the wild animals of the desert.
  They have built siege ramps against its walls,
  torn down its palaces,
  and turned it to a heap of rubble.
¹⁴ Wail, you ships of Tarshish,
  for your harbor is destroyed!

¹⁵ For seventy years, the length of a king's life, Tyre will be forgotten. But then the city will come back to life as in the song about the prostitute:

¹⁶ Take a harp and walk the streets,
  you forgotten harlot.
  Make sweet melody and sing your songs
  so you will be remembered again.

¹⁷ Yes, after seventy years the Lord will revive Tyre. But she will be no different than she was before. She will again be a prostitute to all kingdoms around the world. ¹⁸ But in the end her profits will be given to the Lord. Her wealth will not be hoarded but will provide good food and fine clothing for the Lord's priests.

24

DESTRUCTION OF THE EARTH

1 Look! The Lord is about to destroy the earth
and make it a vast wasteland.
He devastates the surface of the earth
and scatters the people.

2 Priests and laypeople,
servants and masters,
maids and mistresses,
buyers and sellers,
lenders and borrowers,
bankers and debtors—none will be spared.

3 The earth will be completely emptied and looted.
The Lord has spoken!

4 The earth mourns and dries up,
and the land wastes away and withers.
Even the greatest people on earth waste away.

5 The earth suffers for the sins of its people,
for they have twisted God's instructions,
violated his laws,
and broken his everlasting covenant.

6 Therefore, a curse consumes the earth.
Its people must pay the price for their sin.
They are destroyed by fire,
and only a few are left alive.

7 The grapevines waste away,
and there is no new wine.
All the merrymakers sigh and mourn.

8 The cheerful sound of tambourines is stilled;
the happy cries of celebration are heard no more.
The melodious chords of the harp are silent.

9 Gone are the joys of wine and song;
alcoholic drink turns bitter in the mouth.

10 The city writhes in chaos;
every home is locked to keep out intruders.

11 Mobs gather in the streets, crying out for wine.
Joy has turned to gloom.
Gladness has been banished from the land.

12 The city is left in ruins, its gates battered down.

13 Throughout the earth the story is the same—
only a remnant is left,
like the stray olives left on the tree
or the few grapes left on the vine after harvest.

14 But all who are left shout and sing for joy.
Those in the west praise the Lord's majesty.

15 In eastern lands, give glory to the Lord.
In the lands beyond the sea,
praise the name of the Lord,
the God of Israel.

¹⁶ We hear songs of praise from the ends of the earth,
  songs that give glory to the Righteous One!
  But my heart is heavy with grief.
  Weep for me, for I wither away.
  Deceit still prevails,
  and treachery is everywhere.

¹⁷ Terror and traps and snares will be your lot,
  you people of the earth.

¹⁸ Those who flee in terror will fall into a trap,
  and those who escape the trap will be caught in a snare.
  Destruction falls like rain from the heavens;
  the foundations of the earth shake.

¹⁹ The earth has broken up.
  It has utterly collapsed;
  it is violently shaken.

²⁰ The earth staggers like a drunk.
  It trembles like a tent in a storm.
  It falls and will not rise again,
  for the guilt of its rebellion is very heavy.

²¹ In that day the Lord will punish the gods in the heavens
  and the proud rulers of the nations on earth.

²² They will be rounded up and put in prison.
  They will be shut up in prison
  and will finally be punished.

²³ Then the glory of the moon will wane,
  and the brightness of the sun will fade,
  for the Lord of Heaven's Armies
  will rule on Mount Zion.
  He will rule in great glory in Jerusalem,
  in the sight of all the leaders of his people.

PRAISE FOR JUDGMENT AND SALVATION

1 O Lord, I will honor and praise your name,
for you are my God.
You do such wonderful things!
You planned them long ago,
and now you have accomplished them.
2 You turn mighty cities into heaps of ruins.
Cities with strong walls are turned to rubble.
Beautiful palaces in distant lands disappear
and will never be rebuilt.
3 Therefore, strong nations will declare your glory;
ruthless nations will fear you.

4 But you are a tower of refuge to the poor, O Lord,
a tower of refuge to the needy in distress.
You are a refuge from the storm
and a shelter from the heat.
For the oppressive acts of ruthless people
are like a storm beating against a wall,
5 or like the relentless heat of the desert.
But you silence the roar of foreign nations.
As the shade of a cloud cools relentless heat,
so the boastful songs of ruthless people are stilled.
6 In Jerusalem, the Lord of Heaven's Armies
will spread a wonderful feast

for all the people of the world.
It will be a delicious banquet
with clear, well-aged wine and choice meat.
7 There he will remove the cloud of gloom,
the shadow of death that hangs over the earth.
8 He will swallow up death forever!
The Sovereign Lord will wipe away all tears.
He will remove forever all insults and mockery
against his land and people.
The Lord has spoken!
9 In that day the people will proclaim,
"This is our God!

We trusted in him, and he saved us!
This is the Lord, in whom we trusted.
Let us rejoice in the salvation he brings!"
10 For the Lord's hand of blessing will rest on Jerusalem.
But Moab will be crushed.
It will be like straw trampled down and left to rot.
11 God will push down Moab's people
as a swimmer pushes down water with his hands.
He will end their pride and all their evil works.
12 The high walls of Moab will be demolished.
They will be brought down to the ground,
down into the dust.

26

A SONG OF PRAISE TO THE LORD

¹ In that day, everyone in the land of Judah will sing this song:

Our city is strong!
We are surrounded by the walls of God's salvation.
² Open the gates to all who are righteous;
allow the faithful to enter.
³ You will keep in perfect peace
all who trust in you,
all whose thoughts are fixed on you!
⁴ Trust in the Lord always,
for the Lord God is the eternal Rock.
⁵ He humbles the proud
and brings down the arrogant city.
He brings it down to the dust.
⁶ The poor and oppressed trample it underfoot,
and the needy walk all over it.
⁷ But for those who are righteous,
the way is not steep and rough.
You are a God who does what is right,
and you smooth out the path ahead of them.
⁸ Lord, we show our trust in you by obeying your laws;
our heart's desire is to glorify your name.
⁹ In the night I search for you;
in the morning I earnestly seek you.
For only when you come to judge the earth
will people learn what is right.
¹⁰ Your kindness to the wicked
does not make them do good.
Although others do right,
the wicked keep doing wrong
and take no notice of the Lord's majesty.
¹¹ O Lord, they pay no attention
to your upraised fist.
Show them your eagerness to defend your people.
Then they will be ashamed.
Let your fire consume your enemies.
¹² Lord, you will grant us peace;
all we have accomplished is really from you.
¹³ O Lord our God, others have ruled us,
but you alone are the one we worship.
¹⁴ Those we served before are dead and gone.
Their departed spirits will never return!
You attacked them and destroyed them,
and they are long forgotten.
¹⁵ O Lord, you have made our nation great;
yes, you have made us great.
You have extended our borders,
and we give you the glory!

[16] Lord, in distress we searched for you.

We prayed beneath the burden of your discipline.

[17] Just as a pregnant woman

writhes and cries out in pain as she gives birth,

so were we in your presence, Lord.

[18] We, too, writhe in agony,

but nothing comes of our suffering.

We have not given salvation to the earth,

nor brought life into the world.

[19] But those who die in the Lord will live;

their bodies will rise again!

Those who sleep in the earth

will rise up and sing for joy!

For your life-giving light will fall like dew

on your people in the place of the dead!

RESTORATION FOR ISRAEL

[20] Go home, my people,

and lock your doors!

Hide yourselves for a little while

until the Lord's anger has passed.

[21] Look! The Lord is coming from heaven

to punish the people of the earth for their sins.

The earth will no longer hide those

who have been killed.

They will be brought out for all to see.

27

¹ In that day the Lord will take his terrible, swift sword and punish Leviathan, the swiftly moving serpent, the coiling, writhing serpent. He will kill the dragon of the sea.

² "In that day,
sing about the fruitful vineyard.
³ I, the Lord, will watch over it,
watering it carefully.
Day and night I will watch so no one can harm it.
⁴ My anger will be gone.
If I find briers and thorns growing,
I will attack them;
I will burn them up—
⁵ unless they turn to me for help.
Let them make peace with me;
yes, let them make peace with me."
⁶ The time is coming when Jacob's descendants
will take root.
Israel will bud and blossom
and fill the whole earth with fruit!
⁷ Has the Lord struck Israel
as he struck her enemies?
Has he punished her
as he punished them?
⁸ No, but he exiled Israel to call her to account.
She was exiled from her land
as though blown away in a storm from the east.
⁹ The Lord did this to purge Israel's wickedness,
to take away all her sin.
As a result, all the pagan altars
will be crushed to dust.
No Asherah pole or pagan shrine
will be left standing.
¹⁰ The fortified towns will be silent and empty,
the houses abandoned, the streets
overgrown with weeds.
Calves will graze there,
chewing on twigs and branches.
¹¹ The people are like the dead branches of a tree,
broken off and used for kindling beneath the
cooking pots.
Israel is a foolish and stupid nation,
for its people have turned away from God.
Therefore, the one who made them
will show them no pity or mercy.

¹² Yet the time will come when the Lord will gather them together like handpicked grain. One by one he will gather them—from the Euphrates River in the east to the Brook of Egypt in the west. ¹³ In that day the great trumpet will sound. Many who were dying in exile in Assyria and Egypt will return to Jerusalem to worship the Lord on his holy mountain.

28

A MESSAGE ABOUT SAMARIA

¹ What sorrow awaits the proud city of Samaria—
the glorious crown of the drunks of Israel.
It sits at the head of a fertile valley,
but its glorious beauty will fade like a flower.
It is the pride of a people
brought down by wine.

² For the Lord will send a mighty army against it.
Like a mighty hailstorm and a torrential rain,
they will burst upon it like a surging flood
and smash it to the ground.

³ The proud city of Samaria—
the glorious crown of the drunks of Israel—
will be trampled beneath its enemies' feet.

⁴ It sits at the head of a fertile valley,
but its glorious beauty will fade like a flower.
Whoever sees it will snatch it up,
as an early fig is quickly picked and eaten.

⁵ Then at last the Lord of Heaven's Armies
will himself be Israel's glorious crown.
He will be the pride and joy
of the remnant of his people.

⁶ He will give a longing for justice
to their judges.
He will give great courage
to their warriors who stand at the gates.

⁷ Now, however, Israel is led by drunks
who reel with wine and stagger with alcohol.
The priests and prophets stagger with alcohol
and lose themselves in wine.
They reel when they see visions
and stagger as they render decisions.

⁸ Their tables are covered with vomit;
filth is everywhere.

⁹ "Who does the Lord think we are?" they ask.
"Why does he speak to us like this?
Are we little children,
just recently weaned?

¹⁰ He tells us everything over and over—
one line at a time,
one line at a time,
a little here,
and a little there!"

¹¹ So now God will have to speak to his people
through foreign oppressors who
speak a strange language!

¹² God has told his people,
"Here is a place of rest;
let the weary rest here.
This is a place of quiet rest."
But they would not listen.

¹³ So the Lord will spell out his message for them again,
one line at a time,
one line at a time,
a little here,
and a little there,
so that they will stumble and fall.
They will be injured, trapped, and captured.

[14] Therefore, listen to this message from the Lord,
you scoffing rulers in Jerusalem.

[15] You boast, "We have struck a bargain to cheat death
and have made a deal to dodge the grave.
The coming destruction can never touch us,
for we have built a strong refuge made
of lies and deception."

[16] Therefore, this is what the Sovereign Lord says:
"Look! I am placing a foundation stone
in Jerusalem, a firm and tested stone.
It is a precious cornerstone that is safe to build on.
Whoever believes need never be shaken.

[17] I will test you with the measuring line of justice
and the plumb line of righteousness.
Since your refuge is made of lies,
a hailstorm will knock it down.
Since it is made of deception,
a flood will sweep it away.

[18] I will cancel the bargain you made to cheat death,
and I will overturn your deal to dodge the grave.
When the terrible enemy sweeps through,
you will be trampled into the ground.

[19] Again and again that flood will come,
morning after morning,
day and night,
until you are carried away."
This message will bring terror to your people.

[20] The bed you have made is too short to lie on.
The blankets are too narrow to cover you.

[21] The Lord will come as he did
against the Philistines at Mount Perazim
and against the Amorites at Gibeon.
He will come to do a strange thing;
he will come to do an unusual deed:

[22] For the Lord, the Lord of Heaven's Armies,
has plainly said that he is determined
to crush the whole land.
So scoff no more,
or your punishment will be even greater.

[23] Listen to me;
listen, and pay close attention.

[24] Does a farmer always plow and never sow?
Is he forever cultivating the soil and never planting?

[25] Does he not finally plant his seeds—
black cumin, cumin, wheat,
barley, and emmer wheat—
each in its proper way,
and each in its proper place?

[26] The farmer knows just what to do,
for God has given him understanding.

[27] A heavy sledge is never used to thresh black cumin;
rather, it is beaten with a light stick.
A threshing wheel is never rolled on cumin;
instead, it is beaten lightly with a flail.

[28] Grain for bread is easily crushed,
so he doesn't keep on pounding it.
He threshes it under the wheels of a cart,
but he doesn't pulverize it.

[29] The Lord of Heaven's Armies is a wonderful teacher,
and he gives the farmer great wisdom.

29

A MESSAGE ABOUT JERUSALEM

1 "What sorrow awaits Ariel, the City of David.
Year after year you celebrate your feasts.

2 Yet I will bring disaster upon you,
and there will be much weeping and sorrow.
For Jerusalem will become what
her name Ariel means—
an altar covered with blood.

3 I will be your enemy,
surrounding Jerusalem and attacking its walls.
I will build siege towers
and destroy it.

4 Then deep from the earth you will speak;
from low in the dust your words will come.
Your voice will whisper from the ground
like a ghost conjured up from the grave.

5 "But suddenly,
your ruthless enemies will be crushed
like the finest of dust.
Your many attackers will be driven away
like chaff before the wind.
Suddenly, in an instant,

6 I, the Lord of Heaven's Armies, will act for you
with thunder and earthquake and great noise,
with whirlwind and storm and consuming fire.

7 All the nations fighting against Jerusalem will
vanish like a dream!
Those who are attacking her walls
will vanish like a vision in the night.

8 A hungry person dreams of eating
but wakes up still hungry.
A thirsty person dreams of drinking
but is still faint from thirst when morning comes.
So it will be with your enemies,
with those who attack Mount Zion."

9 Are you amazed and incredulous?
Don't you believe it? Then go ahead and be blind.
You are stupid, but not from wine!
You stagger, but not from liquor!

10 For the Lord has poured out on you
a spirit of deep sleep.
He has closed the eyes of
your prophets and visionaries.

11 All the future events in this vision are like a sealed book to them. When you give it to those who can read, they will say, "We can't read it because it is sealed." 12 When you give it to those who cannot read, they will say, "We don't know how to read."

13 And so the Lord says,
   "These people say they are mine.
   They honor me with their lips,
   but their hearts are far from me.
   And their worship of me
   is nothing but man-made rules learned by rote.
14 Because of this, I will once again
   astound these hypocrites
   with amazing wonders.
   The wisdom of the wise will pass away,
   and the intelligence of
   the intelligent will disappear."
15 What sorrow awaits those who try to hide their
   plans from the Lord,
   who do their evil deeds in the dark!
   "The Lord can't see us," they say.
   "He doesn't know what's going on!"
16 How foolish can you be?
   He is the Potter, and he is certainly
   greater than you, the clay!
   Should the created thing
   say of the one who made it,
   "He didn't make me"?
   Does a jar ever say,
   "The potter who made me is stupid"?
17 Soon—and it will not be very long—
   the forests of Lebanon will become a fertile field,

and the fertile field will yield bountiful crops.
18 In that day the deaf will hear
   words read from a book,
   and the blind will see through
   the gloom and darkness.
19 The humble will be filled
   with fresh joy from the Lord.
   The poor will rejoice in the Holy One of Israel.
20 The scoffer will be gone,
   the arrogant will disappear,
   and those who plot evil will be killed.
21 Those who convict the innocent
   by their false testimony will disappear.
   A similar fate awaits those who use
   trickery to pervert justice
   and who tell lies to destroy the innocent.
22 That is why the Lord, who redeemed Abraham,
   says to the people of Israel,
   "My people will no longer be ashamed
   or turn pale with fear.
23 For when they see their many children
   and all the blessings I have given them,
   they will recognize the holiness
   of the Holy One of Jacob.
   They will stand in awe of the God of Israel.
24 Then the wayward will gain understanding,
   and complainers will accept instruction.

30

JUDAH'S WORTHLESS TREATY WITH EGYPT

1 "What sorrow awaits my rebellious children,"
says the Lord.
"You make plans that are contrary to mine.
You make alliances not directed by my Spirit,
thus piling up your sins.

2 For without consulting me,
you have gone down to Egypt for help.
You have put your trust in Pharaoh's protection.
You have tried to hide in his shade.

3 But by trusting Pharaoh, you will be humiliated,
and by depending on him, you will be disgraced.

4 For though his power extends to Zoan
and his officials have arrived in Hanes,

5 all who trust in him will be ashamed.
He will not help you.
Instead, he will disgrace you."

6 This message came to me concerning the animals
in the Negev:
The caravan moves slowly
across the terrible desert to Egypt—
donkeys weighed down with riches
and camels loaded with treasure—
all to pay for Egypt's protection.
They travel through the wilderness,
a place of lionesses and lions,
a place where vipers and poisonous snakes live.
All this, and Egypt will give you nothing in return.

7 Egypt's promises are worthless!
Therefore, I call her Rahab—
the Harmless Dragon.

A WARNING FOR REBELLIOUS JUDAH

8 Now go and write down these words.
Write them in a book.
They will stand until the end of time
as a witness

9 that these people are stubborn rebels
who refuse to pay attention
to the Lord's instructions.

10 They tell the seers,
"Stop seeing visions!"
They tell the prophets,
"Don't tell us what is right.
Tell us nice things.
Tell us lies.

11 Forget all this gloom.
Get off your narrow path.
Stop telling us about your
'Holy One of Israel.'"

¹² This is the reply of the Holy One of Israel:
  "Because you despise what I tell you
  and trust instead in oppression and lies,
¹³ calamity will come upon you suddenly—
  like a bulging wall that bursts and falls.
  In an instant it will collapse
  and come crashing down.
¹⁴ You will be smashed like a piece of pottery—
  shattered so completely that
  there won't be a piece big enough
  to carry coals from a fireplace
  or a little water from the well."
¹⁵ This is what the Sovereign Lord,
  the Holy One of Israel, says:
  "Only in returning to me
   and resting in me will you be saved.
  In quietness and confidence is your strength.
  But you would have none of it.
¹⁶ You said, 'No, we will get our help from Egypt.
  They will give us swift horses for riding into battle.'
  But the only swiftness you are going to see
  is the swiftness of your enemies chasing you!
¹⁷ One of them will chase a thousand of you.

Five of them will make all of you flee.
  You will be left like a lonely flagpole on a hill
  or a tattered banner on a distant mountaintop."

BLESSINGS FOR THE LORD'S PEOPLE

¹⁸ So the Lord must wait for you to come to him
  so he can show you his love and compassion.
  For the Lord is a faithful God.
  Blessed are those who wait for his help.
¹⁹ O people of Zion, who live in Jerusalem,
  you will weep no more.
  He will be gracious if you ask for help.
  He will surely respond to the sound of your cries.
²⁰ Though the Lord gave you adversity for food
  and suffering for drink,
  he will still be with you to teach you.
  You will see your teacher with your own eyes.
²¹ Your own ears will hear him.
  Right behind you a voice will say,
  "This is the way you should go,"
  whether to the right or to the left.
²² Then you will destroy all your silver idols
  and your precious gold images.

You will throw them out like filthy rags,
 saying to them, "Good riddance!"

23 Then the Lord will bless you with rain at planting time. There will be wonderful harvests and plenty of pastureland for your livestock. 24 The oxen and donkeys that till the ground will eat good grain, its chaff blown away by the wind. 25 In that day, when your enemies are slaughtered and the towers fall, there will be streams of water flowing down every mountain and hill. 26 The moon will be as bright as the sun, and the sun will be seven times brighter—like the light of seven days in one! So it will be when the Lord begins to heal his people and cure the wounds he gave them.

27 Look! The Lord is coming from far away,
 burning with anger,
 surrounded by thick, rising smoke.
 His lips are filled with fury;
 his words consume like fire.
28 His hot breath pours out like a flood
 up to the neck of his enemies.
 He will sift out the proud nations for destruction.
 He will bridle them and lead them away to ruin.
29 But the people of God will sing a song of joy,
 like the songs at the holy festivals.
 You will be filled with joy,
 as when a flutist leads a group of pilgrims
 to Jerusalem, the mountain of the Lord—
 to the Rock of Israel.
30 And the Lord will make his majestic voice heard.
 He will display the strength of his mighty arm.
 It will descend with devouring flames,
 with cloudbursts, thunderstorms, and huge hailstones.
31 At the Lord's command, the Assyrians
 will be shattered.
 He will strike them down with his royal scepter.
32 And as the Lord strikes them with
 his rod of punishment,
 his people will celebrate with tambourines and harps.
 Lifting his mighty arm, he will fight the Assyrians.
33 Topheth—the place of burning—
 has long been ready for the Assyrian king;
 the pyre is piled high with wood.
 The breath of the Lord, like fire from a volcano,
 will set it ablaze.

31

THE FUTILITY OF RELYING ON EGYPT

¹ What sorrow awaits those who look
   to Egypt for help,
   trusting their horses, chariots, and charioteers
   and depending on the strength of human armies
   instead of looking to the Lord,
   the Holy One of Israel.
² In his wisdom, the Lord will send great disaster;
   he will not change his mind.
   He will rise against the wicked
   and against their helpers.
³ For these Egyptians are mere humans, not God!
   Their horses are puny flesh,
   not mighty spirits!
   When the Lord raises his fist against them,
   those who help will stumble,
   and those being helped will fall.
   They will all fall down and die together.
⁴ But this is what the Lord has told me:
   "When a strong young lion
   stands growling over a sheep it has killed,
   it is not frightened by the shouts and noise
   of a whole crowd of shepherds.
   In the same way, the Lord of Heaven's Armies
   will come down and fight on Mount Zion.
⁵ The Lord of Heaven's Armies
   will hover over Jerusalem
   and protect it like a bird protecting its nest.
   He will defend and save the city;
   he will pass over it and rescue it."

⁶ Though you are such wicked rebels, my people, come and return to the Lord. ⁷ I know the glorious day will come when each of you will throw away the gold idols and silver images your sinful hands have made.

⁸ "The Assyrians will be destroyed,
   but not by the swords of men.
   The sword of God will strike them,
   and they will panic and flee.
   The strong young Assyrians
   will be taken away as captives.
⁹ Even the strongest will quake with terror,
   and princes will flee when
   they see your battle flags,"
   says the Lord, whose fire burns in Zion,
   whose flame blazes from Jerusalem.

32

ISRAEL'S ULTIMATE DELIVERANCE

1 Look, a righteous king is coming!
And honest princes will rule under him.

2 Each one will be like a shelter from the wind
and a refuge from the storm,
like streams of water in the desert
and the shadow of a great rock in a parched land.

3 Then everyone who has eyes will be able
to see the truth,
and everyone who has ears will be able to hear it.

4 Even the hotheads will be
full of sense and understanding.
Those who stammer will speak out plainly.

5 In that day ungodly fools will not be heroes.
Scoundrels will not be respected.

6 For fools speak foolishness
and make evil plans.
They practice ungodliness
and spread false teachings about the Lord.
They deprive the hungry of food
and give no water to the thirsty.

7 The smooth tricks of scoundrels are evil.
They plot crooked schemes.
They lie to convict the poor,
even when the cause of the poor is just.

8 But generous people plan to do what is generous,
and they stand firm in their generosity.

9 Listen, you women who lie around in ease.
Listen to me, you who are so smug.

10 In a short time—just a little more than a year—
you careless ones will suddenly begin to care.

For your fruit crops will fail,
and the harvest will never take place.

11 Tremble, you women of ease;
throw off your complacency.
Strip off your pretty clothes,
and put on burlap to show your grief.

12 Beat your breasts in sorrow for your bountiful farms
and your fruitful grapevines.

13 For your land will be overgrown
with thorns and briers.
Your joyful homes and happy towns will be gone.

14 The palace and the city will be deserted,
and busy towns will be empty.
Wild donkeys will frolic and flocks will graze
in the empty forts and watchtowers

15 until at last the Spirit is poured out
on us from heaven.
Then the wilderness will become a fertile field,
and the fertile field will yield bountiful crops.

16 Justice will rule in the wilderness
and righteousness in the fertile field.

17 And this righteousness will bring peace.
Yes, it will bring quietness and confidence forever.

18 My people will live in safety, quietly at home.
They will be at rest.

19 Even if the forest should be destroyed
and the city torn down,

20 the Lord will greatly bless his people.
Wherever they plant seed, bountiful crops
will spring up.
Their cattle and donkeys will graze freely.

33

A MESSAGE ABOUT ASSYRIA

1 What sorrow awaits you Assyrians,
who have destroyed others
but have never been destroyed yourselves.
You betray others,
but you have never been betrayed.
When you are done destroying,
you will be destroyed.
When you are done betraying,
you will be betrayed.

2 But Lord, be merciful to us,
for we have waited for you.
Be our strong arm each day
and our salvation in times of trouble.

3 The enemy runs at the sound of your voice.
When you stand up, the nations flee!

4 Just as caterpillars and
locusts strip the fields and vines,
so the fallen army of Assyria will be stripped!

5 Though the Lord is very great and lives in heaven,
he will make Jerusalem his home
of justice and righteousness.

6 In that day he will be your sure foundation,
providing a rich store of salvation,
wisdom, and knowledge.
The fear of the Lord will be your treasure.

7 But now your brave warriors weep in public.
Your ambassadors of peace cry
in bitter disappointment.

8 Your roads are deserted;
no one travels them anymore.
The Assyrians have broken their peace treaty
and care nothing for the promises they made
before witnesses.
They have no respect for anyone.

9 The land of Israel wilts in mourning.
Lebanon withers with shame.
The plain of Sharon is now a wilderness.
Bashan and Carmel have been plundered.

10 But the Lord says: "Now I will stand up.
Now I will show my power and might.

11 You Assyrians produce nothing but
dry grass and stubble.
Your own breath will turn to fire and consume you.

12 Your people will be burned up completely,
like thornbushes cut down and tossed in a fire.

13 Listen to what I have done, you nations far away!
And you that are near,
acknowledge my might!"

14 The sinners in Jerusalem shake with fear.
Terror seizes the godless.
"Who can live with this devouring fire?" they cry.
"Who can survive this all-consuming fire?"

¹⁵ Those who are honest and fair,
who refuse to profit by fraud,
who stay far away from bribes,
who refuse to listen to those who plot murder,
who shut their eyes to all enticement to do wrong—
¹⁶ these are the ones who will dwell on high.
The rocks of the mountains will be their fortress.
Food will be supplied to them,
and they will have water in abundance.
¹⁷ Your eyes will see the king in all his splendor,
and you will see a land that stretches into the distance.
¹⁸ You will think back to this time of terror, asking,
"Where are the Assyrian officers
who counted our towers?
Where are the bookkeepers
who recorded the plunder taken from our fallen city?"
¹⁹ You will no longer see these fierce, violent people
with their strange, unknown language.
²⁰ Instead, you will see Zion as a place of holy festivals.
You will see Jerusalem, a city quiet and secure.
It will be like a tent whose ropes are taut
and whose stakes are firmly fixed.
²¹ The Lord will be our Mighty One.
He will be like a wide river of protection
that no enemy can cross,
that no enemy ship can sail upon.
²² For the Lord is our judge,
our lawgiver, and our king.
He will care for us and save us.
²³ The enemies' sails hang loose
on broken masts with useless tackle.
Their treasure will be divided by the people of God.
Even the lame will take their share!
²⁴ The people of Israel will no longer say,
"We are sick and helpless,"
for the Lord will forgive their sins.

34

A MESSAGE FOR THE NATIONS

¹ Come here and listen, O nations of the earth.
Let the world and everything in it hear my words.

² For the Lord is enraged against the nations.
His fury is against all their armies.
He will completely destroy them,
dooming them to slaughter.

³ Their dead will be left unburied,
and the stench of rotting bodies will fill the land.
The mountains will flow with their blood.

⁴ The heavens above will melt away
and disappear like a rolled-up scroll.
The stars will fall from the sky
like withered leaves from a grapevine,
or shriveled figs from a fig tree.

⁵ And when my sword has finished
its work in the heavens,
it will fall upon Edom,
the nation I have marked for destruction.

⁶ The sword of the Lord is drenched with blood
and covered with fat—
with the blood of lambs and goats,
with the fat of rams prepared for sacrifice.
Yes, the Lord will offer a
sacrifice in the city of Bozrah.
He will make a mighty slaughter in Edom.

⁷ Even men as strong as wild oxen will die—
the young men alongside the veterans.
The land will be soaked with blood
and the soil enriched with fat.

⁸ For it is the day of the Lord's revenge,
the year when Edom will be paid back
for all it did to Israel.

⁹ The streams of Edom
will be filled with burning pitch,
and the ground will be covered with fire.

¹⁰ This judgment on Edom will never end;
the smoke of its burning will rise forever.
The land will lie deserted
from generation to generation.
No one will live there anymore.

¹¹ It will be haunted by the desert owl
and the screech owl,
the great owl and the raven.
For God will measure that land carefully;
he will measure it for chaos and destruction.

¹² It will be called the Land of Nothing,
and all its nobles will soon be gone.

¹³ Thorns will overrun its palaces;
nettles and thistles will grow in its forts.
The ruins will become a haunt for jackals
and a home for owls.

¹⁴ Desert animals will mingle there with hyenas,
their howls filling the night.
Wild goats will bleat at one another among the ruins,
and night creatures will come there to rest.

¹⁵ There the owl will make her nest and lay her eggs.
She will hatch her young
and cover them with her wings.
And the buzzards will come, each one with its mate.

¹⁶ Search the book of the Lord,
and see what he will do.
Not one of these birds and animals will be missing,
and none will lack a mate,
for the Lord has promised this.
His Spirit will make it all come true.

¹⁷ He has surveyed and divided the land
and deeded it over to those creatures.
They will possess it forever,
from generation to generation.

35

HOPE FOR RESTORATION

1 Even the wilderness and desert will
be glad in those days.
The wasteland will rejoice and
blossom with spring crocuses.

2 Yes, there will be an abundance of flowers
and singing and joy!
The deserts will become as green as the mountains
of Lebanon,
as lovely as Mount Carmel or the plain of Sharon.
There the Lord will display his glory,
the splendor of our God.

3 With this news,
strengthen those who have tired hands,

4 and encourage those who have weak knees.
Say to those with fearful hearts,
"Be strong, and do not fear,
for your God is coming to destroy your enemies.
He is coming to save you."

5 And when he comes,
he will open the eyes of the blind
and unplug the ears of the deaf.

6 The lame will leap like a deer,
and those who cannot speak will sing for joy!
Springs will gush forth in the wilderness,
and streams will water the wasteland.

7 The parched ground will become a pool,
and springs of water will satisfy the thirsty land.
Marsh grass and reeds and rushes will flourish
where desert jackals once lived.

8 And a great road will go through
that once deserted land.
It will be named the Highway of Holiness.
Evil-minded people will never travel on it.
It will be only for those who walk in God's ways;
fools will never walk there.

9 Lions will not lurk along its course,
nor any other ferocious beasts.
There will be no other dangers.
Only the redeemed will walk on it.

10 Those who have been ransomed by
the Lord will return.
They will enter Jerusalem singing,
crowned with everlasting joy.
Sorrow and mourning will disappear,
and they will be filled with joy and gladness.

36

ASSYRIA INVADES JUDAH

[1] In the fourteenth year of King Hezekiah's reign, King Sennacherib of Assyria came to attack the fortified towns of Judah and conquered them. [2] Then the king of Assyria sent his chief of staff from Lachish with a huge army to confront King Hezekiah in Jerusalem. The Assyrians took up a position beside the aqueduct that feeds water into the upper pool, near the road leading to the field where cloth is washed. [3] These are the officials who went out to meet with them: Eliakim son of Hilkiah, the palace administrator; Shebna the court secretary; and Joah son of Asaph, the royal historian.

SENNACHERIB THREATENS JERUSALEM

[4] Then the Assyrian king's chief of staff told them to give this message to Hezekiah:

"This is what the great king of Assyria says: What are you trusting in that makes you so confident? [5] Do you think that mere words can substitute for military skill and strength? Who are you counting on, that you have rebelled against me? [6] On Egypt? If you lean on Egypt, it will be like a reed that splinters beneath your weight and pierces your hand. Pharaoh, the king of Egypt, is completely unreliable! [7] "But perhaps you will say to me, 'We are trusting in the Lord our God!' But isn't he the one who was insulted by Hezekiah? Didn't Hezekiah tear down his shrines and altars and make everyone in Judah and Jerusalem worship only at the altar here in Jerusalem? [8] "I'll tell you what! Strike a bargain with my master, the king of Assyria. I will give you 2,000 horses if you can find that many men to ride on them! [9] With your tiny army, how can you think of challenging even the weakest contingent of my master's troops, even with the help of Egypt's chariots and charioteers? [10] What's more, do you think we have invaded your land without the Lord's direction? The Lord himself told us, 'Attack this land and destroy it!'"

[11] Then Eliakim, Shebna, and Joah said to the Assyrian chief of staff, "Please speak to us in Aramaic, for we understand it well. Don't speak in Hebrew,for the people on the wall will hear." [12] But Sennacherib's chief of staff replied, "Do you think my master sent this message only to you and your master? He wants all the people to hear it, for when we put this city under siege, they will suffer along with you. They will be so hungry and thirsty that they will eat their own dung and drink their own urine." [13] Then the chief of staff stood and shouted in Hebrew to the people on the wall, "Listen to this message from the great king of Assyria! [14] This is what the king says: Don't let Hezekiah deceive you. He will never be able to rescue you. [15] Don't let him fool you into trusting in the Lord by saying, 'The Lord will surely rescue us. This city will never fall into the hands of the Assyrian king!' [16] "Don't listen to Hezekiah! These are the terms the king of Assyria is offering: Make peace with me—open the gates and come out. Then each of you can continue eating from your own grapevine and fig tree and drinking from your own well. [17] Then I will arrange to take you to another land like this one—a land of grain and new wine, bread and vineyards. [18] "Don't let Hezekiah mislead you by saying, 'The Lord will rescue us!' Have the gods of any other nations ever saved their people from the king of Assyria? [19] What happened to the gods of Hamath and Arpad? And what about the gods of Sepharvaim? Did any god rescue Samaria from my power? [20] What god of any nation has ever been able to save its people from my power? So what makes you think that the Lord can rescue Jerusalem from me?" [21] But the people were silent and did not utter a word because Hezekiah had commanded them, "Do not answer him." [22] Then Eliakim son of Hilkiah, the palace administrator; Shebna the court secretary; and Joah son of Asaph, the royal historian, went back to Hezekiah. They tore their clothes in despair, and they went in to see the king and told him what the Assyrian chief of staff had said.

37

HEZEKIAH SEEKS THE LORD'S HELP

[1] When King Hezekiah heard their report, he tore his clothes and put on burlap and went into the Temple of the Lord. [2] And he sent Eliakim the palace administrator, Shebna the court secretary, and the leading priests, all dressed in burlap, to the prophet Isaiah son of Amoz. [3] They told him, "This is what King Hezekiah says: Today is a day of trouble, insults, and disgrace. It is like when a child is ready to be born, but the mother has no strength to deliver the baby. [4] But perhaps the Lord your God has heard the Assyrian chief of staff, sent by the king to defy the living God, and will punish him for his words. Oh, pray for those of us who are left!"

[5] After King Hezekiah's officials delivered the king's message to Isaiah, [6] the prophet replied, "Say to your master, 'This is what the Lord says: Do not be disturbed by this blasphemous speech against me from the Assyrian king's messengers. [7] Listen! I myself will move against him, and the king will receive a message that he is needed at home. So he will return to his land, where I will have him killed with a sword.'" [8] Meanwhile, the Assyrian chief of staff left Jerusalem and went to consult the king of Assyria, who had left Lachish and was attacking Libnah. [9] Soon afterward King Sennacherib received word that King Tirhakah of Ethiopia was leading an army to fight against him. Before leaving to meet the attack, he sent messengers back to Hezekiah in Jerusalem with this message: [10] "This message is for King Hezekiah of Judah. Don't let your God, in whom you trust, deceive you with promises that Jerusalem will not be captured by the king of Assyria. [11] You know perfectly well what the kings of Assyria have done wherever they have gone. They have completely destroyed everyone who stood in their way! Why should you be any different? [12] Have the gods of other nations rescued them—such nations as Gozan, Haran, Rezeph, and the people of Eden who were in Tel-assar? My predecessors destroyed them all! [13] What happened to the king of Hamath and the king of Arpad? What happened to the kings of Sepharvaim, Hena, and Ivvah?" [14] After Hezekiah received the letter from the messengers and read it, he went up to the Lord's Temple and spread it out before the Lord. [15] And Hezekiah prayed this prayer before the Lord: [16] "O Lord of Heaven's Armies, God of Israel, you are enthroned between the mighty cherubim! You alone are God of all the kingdoms of the earth. You alone created the heavens and the earth. [17] Bend down, O Lord, and listen! Open your eyes, O Lord, and see! Listen to Sennacherib's words of defiance against the living God. [18] "It is true, Lord, that the kings of Assyria have destroyed all these nations. [19] And they have thrown the gods of these nations into the fire and burned them. But of course the Assyrians could destroy them! They were not gods at all—only idols of wood and stone shaped by human hands. [20] Now, O Lord our God, rescue us from his power; then all the kingdoms of the earth will know that you alone, O Lord, are God."

ISAIAH PREDICTS JUDAH'S DELIVERANCE

21 Then Isaiah son of Amoz sent this message to Hezekiah: "This is what the Lord, the God of Israel, says: Because you prayed about King Sennacherib of Assyria, 22 the Lord has spoken this word against him:

"The virgin daughter of Zion
despises you and laughs at you.
The daughter of Jerusalem
shakes her head in derision as you flee.
23 "Whom have you been defying and ridiculing?
Against whom did you raise your voice?
At whom did you look with such haughty eyes?
It was the Holy One of Israel!
24 By your messengers you have defied the Lord.
You have said, 'With my many chariots
I have conquered the highest mountains—
yes, the remotest peaks of Lebanon.
I have cut down its tallest cedars
and its finest cypress trees.
I have reached its farthest heights
and explored its deepest forests.
25 I have dug wells in many foreign lands
and refreshed myself with their water.
With the sole of my foot,
I stopped up all the rivers of Egypt!'
26 "But have you not heard?
I decided this long ago.
Long ago I planned it,
and now I am making it happen.
I planned for you to crush fortified cities
into heaps of rubble.
27 That is why their people have so little power
and are so frightened and confused.
They are as weak as grass,
as easily trampled as tender green shoots.
They are like grass sprouting on a housetop,
scorched before it can grow lush and tall.

28 "But I know you well—where you stay
and when you come and go.
I know the way you have raged against me.
29 And because of your raging against me
and your arrogance, which I have heard for myself,
I will put my hook in your nose
and my bit in your mouth.
I will make you return
by the same road on which you came."

30 Then Isaiah said to Hezekiah, "Here is the proof that what I say is true:

"This year you will eat only
what grows up by itself,
and next year you will eat
what springs up from that.
But in the third year you will plant crops
and harvest them;
you will tend vineyards and eat their fruit.
31 And you who are left in Judah,
who have escaped the ravages of the siege,
will put roots down in your own soil
and grow up and flourish.
32 For a remnant of my people will
spread out from Jerusalem,
a group of survivors from Mount Zion.
The passionate commitment of the
Lord of Heaven's Armies
will make this happen!

33 "And this is what the Lord says about the king of Assyria:

"'His armies will not enter Jerusalem.
They will not even shoot an arrow at it.
They will not march outside
its gates with their shields
nor build banks of earth against its walls.

³⁴ The king will return to his own country
by the same road on which he came.
He will not enter this city,'
says the Lord.
³⁵ 'For my own honor and for the
sake of my servant David,
I will defend this city and protect it.'"

³⁶ That night the angel of the Lord went out to the Assyrian camp and killed 185,000 Assyrian soldiers. When the surviving Assyrians woke up the next morning, they found corpses everywhere. ³⁷ Then King Sennacherib of Assyria broke camp and returned to his own land. He went home to his capital of Nineveh and stayed there. ³⁸ One day while he was worshiping in the temple of his god Nisroch, his sons Adrammelech and Sharezer killed him with their swords. They then escaped to the land of Ararat, and another son, Esarhaddon, became the next king of Assyria.

38

HEZEKIAH'S SICKNESS AND RECOVERY

[1] About that time Hezekiah became deathly ill, and the prophet Isaiah son of Amoz went to visit him. He gave the king this message: "This is what the Lord says: 'Set your affairs in order, for you are going to die. You will not recover from this illness.'" [2] When Hezekiah heard this, he turned his face to the wall and prayed to the Lord, [3] "Remember, O Lord, how I have always been faithful to you and have served you single-mindedly, always doing what pleases you." Then he broke down and wept bitterly. [4] Then this message came to Isaiah from the Lord: [5] "Go back to Hezekiah and tell him, 'This is what the Lord, the God of your ancestor David, says: I have heard your prayer and seen your tears. I will add fifteen years to your life, [6] and I will rescue you and this city from the king of Assyria. Yes, I will defend this city. [7] "'And this is the sign from the Lord to prove that he will do as he promised: [8] I will cause the sun's shadow to move ten steps backward on the sundial of Ahaz!'" So the shadow on the sundial moved backward ten steps.

HEZEKIAH'S POEM OF PRAISE

⁹ When King Hezekiah was well again,
he wrote this poem:

¹⁰ I said, "In the prime of my life,
must I now enter the place of the dead?
Am I to be robbed of the rest of my years?"

¹¹ I said, "Never again will I see the Lord God
while still in the land of the living.
Never again will I see my friends
or be with those who live in this world.

¹² My life has been blown away
like a shepherd's tent in a storm.
It has been cut short,
as when a weaver cuts cloth from a loom.
Suddenly, my life was over.

¹³ I waited patiently all night,
but I was torn apart as though by lions.
Suddenly, my life was over.

¹⁴ Delirious, I chattered like a swallow or a crane,
and then I moaned like a mourning dove.
My eyes grew tired of looking to heaven for help.
I am in trouble, Lord. Help me!"

¹⁵ But what could I say?
For he himself sent this sickness.
Now I will walk humbly throughout my years
because of this anguish I have felt.

¹⁶ Lord, your discipline is good,
for it leads to life and health.
You restore my health
and allow me to live!

¹⁷ Yes, this anguish was good for me,
for you have rescued me from death
and forgiven all my sins.

¹⁸ For the dead cannot praise you;
they cannot raise their voices in praise.
Those who go down to the grave
can no longer hope in your faithfulness.

¹⁹ Only the living can praise you as I do today.
Each generation tells of your
faithfulness to the next.

²⁰ Think of it—the Lord is ready to heal me!
I will sing his praises with instruments
every day of my life
in the Temple of the Lord.

²¹ Isaiah had said to Hezekiah's servants, "Make an ointment from figs and spread it over the boil, and Hezekiah will recover." ²² And Hezekiah had asked, "What sign will prove that I will go to the Temple of the Lord?"

39

ENVOYS FROM BABYLON

[1] Soon after this, Merodach-baladan son of Baladan, king of Babylon, sent Hezekiah his best wishes and a gift. He had heard that Hezekiah had been very sick and that he had recovered. [2] Hezekiah was delighted with the Babylonian envoys and showed them everything in his treasure-houses—the silver, the gold, the spices, and the aromatic oils. He also took them to see his armory and showed them everything in his royal treasuries! There was nothing in his palace or kingdom that Hezekiah did not show them. [3] Then Isaiah the prophet went to King Hezekiah and asked him, "What did those men want? Where were they from?" Hezekiah replied, "They came from the distant land of Babylon." [4] "What did they see in your palace?" asked Isaiah. "They saw everything," Hezekiah replied. "I showed them everything I own—all my royal treasures." [5] Then Isaiah said to Hezekiah, "Listen to this message from the Lord of Heaven's Armies: [6] 'The time is coming when everything in your palace—all the treasures stored up by your ancestors until now—will be carried off to Babylon. Nothing will be left,' says the Lord. [7] 'Some of your very own sons will be taken away into exile. They will become eunuchs who will serve in the palace of Babylon's king.'" [8] Then Hezekiah said to Isaiah, "This message you have given me from the Lord is good." For the king was thinking, "At least there will be peace and security during my lifetime."

40

COMFORT FOR GOD'S PEOPLE

1 "Comfort, comfort my people,"
says your God.
2 "Speak tenderly to Jerusalem.
Tell her that her sad days are gone
and her sins are pardoned.
Yes, the Lord has punished her twice over
for all her sins."
3 Listen! It's the voice of someone shouting,
"Clear the way through the wilderness
for the Lord!
Make a straight highway through the wasteland
for our God!
4 Fill in the valleys,
and level the mountains and hills.
Straighten the curves,
and smooth out the rough places.
5 Then the glory of the Lord will be revealed,
and all people will see it together.
The Lord has spoken!"
6 A voice said, "Shout!"
I asked, "What should I shout?"

"Shout that people are like the grass.
Their beauty fades as quickly
as the flowers in a field.
7 The grass withers and the flowers fade
beneath the breath of the Lord.
And so it is with people.
8 The grass withers and the flowers fade,
but the word of our God stands forever."
9 O Zion, messenger of good news,
shout from the mountaintops!
Shout it louder, O Jerusalem.
Shout, and do not be afraid.
Tell the towns of Judah,
"Your God is coming!"
10 Yes, the Sovereign Lord is coming in power.
He will rule with a powerful arm.
See, he brings his reward with him as he comes.
11 He will feed his flock like a shepherd.
He will carry the lambs in his arms,
holding them close to his heart.
He will gently lead the mother
sheep with their young.

THE LORD HAS NO EQUAL

12 Who else has held the oceans in his hand?
Who has measured off the heavens with his fingers?
Who else knows the weight of the earth
or has weighed the mountains and hills on a scale?

13 Who is able to advise the Spirit of the Lord?
Who knows enough to give him
advice or teach him?

14 Has the Lord ever needed anyone's advice?
Does he need instruction about what is good?
Did someone teach him what is right
or show him the path of justice?

15 No, for all the nations of the world
are but a drop in the bucket.
They are nothing more
than dust on the scales.
He picks up the whole earth
as though it were a grain of sand.

16 All the wood in Lebanon's forests
and all Lebanon's animals would not be enough
to make a burnt offering worthy of our God.

17 The nations of the world are worth nothing to him.
In his eyes they count for less than nothing—
mere emptiness and froth.

18 To whom can you compare God?
What image can you find to resemble him?

19 Can he be compared to an idol formed in a mold,
overlaid with gold,
and decorated with silver chains?

20 Or if people are too poor for that,
they might at least choose wood that won't decay
and a skilled craftsman
to carve an image that won't fall down!

21 Haven't you heard? Don't you understand?
Are you deaf to the words of God—
the words he gave before the world began?

Are you so ignorant?

22 God sits above the circle of the earth.
The people below seem like grasshoppers to him!
He spreads out the heavens like a curtain
and makes his tent from them.

23 He judges the great people of the world
and brings them all to nothing.

24 They hardly get started, barely taking root,
when he blows on them and they wither.
The wind carries them off like chaff.

25 "To whom will you compare me?
Who is my equal?" asks the Holy One.

26 Look up into the heavens.
Who created all the stars?
He brings them out like an army, one after another,
calling each by its name.
Because of his great power
and incomparable strength,

not a single one is missing.

27 O Jacob, how can you say the Lord
does not see your troubles?
O Israel, how can you say God ignores your rights?

28 Have you never heard?
Have you never understood?
The Lord is the everlasting God,
the Creator of all the earth.
He never grows weak or weary.
No one can measure the depths of his understanding.

29 He gives power to the weak
and strength to the powerless.

30 Even youths will become weak and tired,
and young men will fall in exhaustion.

31 But those who trust in the Lord will find new strength.
They will soar high on wings like eagles.
They will run and not grow weary.
They will walk and not faint.

41

GOD'S HELP FOR ISRAEL

1 "Listen in silence before me,
you lands beyond the sea.
Bring your strongest arguments.
Come now and speak.
The court is ready for your case.

2 "Who has stirred up this king from the east,
rightly calling him to God's service?
Who gives this man victory over many nations
and permits him to trample their kings underfoot?
With his sword, he reduces armies to dust.
With his bow, he scatters them
like chaff before the wind.

3 He chases them away and goes on safely,
though he is walking over unfamiliar ground.

4 Who has done such mighty deeds,
summoning each new generation from
the beginning of time?
It is I, the Lord, the First and the Last.
I alone am he."

5 The lands beyond the sea watch in fear.
Remote lands tremble and mobilize for war.

6 The idol makers encourage one another,
saying to each other, "Be strong!"

7 The carver encourages the goldsmith,
and the molder helps at the anvil.

"Good," they say. "It's coming along fine."
Carefully they join the parts together,
then fasten the thing in place so it won't fall over.

8 "But as for you, Israel my servant,
Jacob my chosen one,
descended from Abraham my friend,

9 I have called you back from the ends of the earth,
saying, 'You are my servant.'
For I have chosen you
and will not throw you away.

10 Don't be afraid, for I am with you.
Don't be discouraged, for I am your God.
I will strengthen you and help you.
I will hold you up with my victorious right hand.

11 "See, all your angry enemies lie there,
confused and humiliated.
Anyone who opposes you will die
and come to nothing.

12 You will look in vain
for those who tried to conquer you.
Those who attack you
will come to nothing.

13 For I hold you by your right hand—
I, the Lord your God.
And I say to you,
'Don't be afraid. I am here to help you.

14 Though you are a lowly worm, O Jacob,
don't be afraid, people of Israel, for I will help you.
I am the Lord, your Redeemer.
I am the Holy One of Israel.'

15 You will be a new threshing instrument
with many sharp teeth.
You will tear your enemies apart,
making chaff of mountains.

16 You will toss them into the air,
and the wind will blow them all away;
a whirlwind will scatter them.
Then you will rejoice in the Lord.
You will glory in the Holy One of Israel.

17 "When the poor and needy search for water and
there is none,
and their tongues are parched from thirst,
then I, the Lord, will answer them.
I, the God of Israel, will never abandon them.

18 I will open up rivers for them on the high plateaus.
I will give them fountains of water in the valleys.
I will fill the desert with pools of water.
Rivers fed by springs will flow across
the parched ground.

19 I will plant trees in the barren desert—
cedar, acacia, myrtle, olive, cypress, fir, and pine.

20 I am doing this so all who see this miracle
will understand what it means—
that it is the Lord who has done this,
the Holy One of Israel who created it.

21 "Present the case for your idols,"
says the Lord.

22 "Let them show what they can do,"
says the King of Israel.
"Let them try to tell us what happened long ago
so that we may consider the evidence.
Or let them tell us what the future holds,
so we can know what's going to happen.

23 Yes, tell us what will occur in the days ahead.
Then we will know you are gods.
In fact, do anything—good or bad!
Do something that will amaze and frighten us.

24 But no! You are less than nothing
and can do nothing at all.
Those who choose you pollute themselves.

25 "But I have stirred up a leader who will approach
from the north.
From the east he will call on my name.
I will give him victory over kings and princes.
He will trample them as a potter treads on clay.

26 "Who told you from the beginning
that this would happen?
Who predicted this,
making you admit that he was right?
No one said a word!

27 I was the first to tell Zion,
'Look! Help is on the way!'
I will send Jerusalem
a messenger with good news.

28 Not one of your idols told you this.
Not one gave any answer when I asked.

29 See, they are all foolish, worthless things.
All your idols are as empty as the wind.

42

THE LORD'S CHOSEN SERVANT

1 "Look at my servant, whom I strengthen.
He is my chosen one, who pleases me.
I have put my Spirit upon him.
He will bring justice to the nations.

2 He will not shout
or raise his voice in public.

3 He will not crush the weakest reed
or put out a flickering candle.
He will bring justice to
all who have been wronged.

4 He will not falter or lose heart
until justice prevails throughout the earth.
Even distant lands beyond the sea
will wait for his instruction."

5 God, the Lord, created the heavens and
stretched them out.
He created the earth and everything in it.

He gives breath to everyone,
life to everyone who walks the earth.
And it is he who says,

6 "I, the Lord, have called you
to demonstrate my righteousness.
I will take you by the hand and guard you,
and I will give you to my people, Israel,
as a symbol of my covenant with them.
And you will be a light to guide the nations.

7 You will open the eyes of the blind.
You will free the captives from prison,
releasing those who sit in dark dungeons.

8 "I am the Lord; that is my name!
I will not give my glory to anyone else,
nor share my praise with carved idols.

9 Everything I prophesied has come true,
and now I will prophesy again.
I will tell you the future before it happens."

A SONG OF PRAISE TO THE LORD

¹⁰ Sing a new song to the Lord!
Sing his praises from the ends of the earth!
Sing, all you who sail the seas,
all you who live in distant coastlands.

¹¹ Join in the chorus, you desert towns;
let the villages of Kedar rejoice!
Let the people of Sela sing for joy;
shout praises from the mountaintops!

¹² Let the whole world glorify the Lord;
let it sing his praise.

¹³ The Lord will march forth like a mighty hero;
he will come out like a warrior, full of fury.
He will shout his battle cry and crush all his enemies.

¹⁴ He will say, "I have long been silent;
yes, I have restrained myself.

But now, like a woman in labor,
I will cry and groan and pant.

¹⁵ I will level the mountains and hills
and blight all their greenery.
I will turn the rivers into dry land
and will dry up all the pools.

¹⁶ I will lead blind Israel down a new path,
guiding them along an unfamiliar way.
I will brighten the darkness before them
and smooth out the road ahead of them.
Yes, I will indeed do these things;
I will not forsake them.

¹⁷ But those who trust in idols,
who say, 'You are our gods,'
will be turned away in shame.

ISRAEL'S FAILURE TO LISTEN AND SEE

¹⁸ "Listen, you who are deaf!
Look and see, you blind!

¹⁹ Who is as blind as my own people, my servant?
Who is as deaf as my messenger?
Who is as blind as my chosen people,
the servant of the Lord?

²⁰ You see and recognize what is right
but refuse to act on it.
You hear with your ears,
but you don't really listen."

²¹ Because he is righteous,
the Lord has exalted his glorious law.

²² But his own people have been
robbed and plundered,
enslaved, imprisoned, and trapped.

They are fair game for anyone
and have no one to protect them,
no one to take them back home.

²³ Who will hear these lessons from the past
and see the ruin that awaits you in the future?

²⁴ Who allowed Israel to be robbed and hurt?
It was the Lord, against whom we sinned,
for the people would not walk in his path,
nor would they obey his law.

²⁵ Therefore, he poured out his fury on them
and destroyed them in battle.
They were enveloped in flames,
but they still refused to understand.
They were consumed by fire,
but they did not learn their lesson.

43

THE SAVIOR OF ISRAEL

1 But now, O Jacob, listen to the Lord who created you.
O Israel, the one who formed you says,
"Do not be afraid, for I have ransomed you.
I have called you by name; you are mine.

2 When you go through deep waters,
I will be with you.
When you go through rivers of difficulty,
you will not drown.
When you walk through the fire of oppression,
you will not be burned up;
the flames will not consume you.

3 For I am the Lord, your God,
the Holy One of Israel, your Savior.
I gave Egypt as a ransom for your freedom;
I gave Ethiopia and Seba in your place.

4 Others were given in exchange for you.
I traded their lives for yours
because you are precious to me.
You are honored, and I love you.

5 "Do not be afraid, for I am with you.
I will gather you and your children from east and west.

6 I will say to the north and south,
'Bring my sons and daughters back to Israel
from the distant corners of the earth.

7 Bring all who claim me as their God,
for I have made them for my glory.

It was I who created them.'"

⁸ Bring out the people who have eyes but are blind,
who have ears but are deaf.

⁹ Gather the nations together!
Assemble the peoples of the world!
Which of their idols has
ever foretold such things?
Which can predict what will happen tomorrow?
Where are the witnesses of such predictions?
Who can verify that they spoke the truth?

¹⁰ "But you are my witnesses,
O Israel!" says the Lord.
"You are my servant.
You have been chosen to know me, believe in me,
and understand that I alone am God.
There is no other God—
there never has been, and there never will be.

¹¹ I, yes I, am the Lord,
and there is no other Savior.

¹² First I predicted your rescue,
then I saved you and proclaimed it to the world.
No foreign god has ever done this.
You are witnesses that I am the only God,"
says the Lord.

¹³ "From eternity to eternity I am God.
No one can snatch anyone out of my hand.
No one can undo what I have done."

THE LORD'S PROMISE OF VICTORY

¹⁴ This is what the Lord says—your Redeemer, the Holy One of Israel:

"For your sakes I will send
an army against Babylon,
forcing the Babylonians to flee in
those ships they are so proud of.
¹⁵ I am the Lord, your Holy One,
Israel's Creator and King.
¹⁶ I am the Lord, who opened a way through
the waters, making a dry path through the sea.
¹⁷ I called forth the mighty army of Egypt
with all its chariots and horses.
I drew them beneath the waves, and they drowned,
their lives snuffed out like a smoldering candlewick.
¹⁸ "But forget all that—
it is nothing compared to what I am going to do.
¹⁹ For I am about to do something new.
See, I have already begun! Do you not see it?
I will make a pathway through the wilderness.
I will create rivers in the dry wasteland.
²⁰ The wild animals in the fields will thank me,
the jackals and owls, too,
for giving them water in the desert.
Yes, I will make rivers in the dry wasteland
so my chosen people can be refreshed.

²¹ I have made Israel for myself,
and they will someday honor
me before the whole world.
²² "But, dear family of Jacob,
you refuse to ask for my help.
You have grown tired of me, O Israel!
²³ You have not brought me sheep
or goats for burnt offerings.
You have not honored me with sacrifices,
though I have not burdened and wearied you
with requests for grain offerings and frankincense.
²⁴ You have not brought me fragrant calamus
or pleased me with the fat from sacrifices.
Instead, you have burdened me with your sins
and wearied me with your faults.
²⁵ "I—yes, I alone—will blot out
your sins for my own sake
and will never think of them again.
²⁶ Let us review the situation together,
and you can present your case
to prove your innocence.
²⁷ From the very beginning, your
first ancestor sinned against me;
all your leaders broke my laws.
²⁸ That is why I have disgraced your priests;
I have decreed complete destruction for Jacob
and shame for Israel.

44

¹ "But now, listen to me, Jacob my servant,
Israel my chosen one.
² The Lord who made you and helps you says:
Do not be afraid, O Jacob, my servant,
O dear Israel, my chosen one.
³ For I will pour out water to quench your thirst
and to irrigate your parched fields.
And I will pour out my Spirit on your descendants,
and my blessing on your children.
⁴ They will thrive like watered grass,
like willows on a riverbank.
⁵ Some will proudly claim, 'I belong to the Lord.'
Others will say, 'I am a descendant of Jacob.'
Some will write the Lord's name on their hands
and will take the name of Israel as their own."

THE FOOLISHNESS OF IDOLS

⁶ This is what the Lord says—Israel's King and
Redeemer, the Lord of Heaven's Armies:
"I am the First and the Last;
there is no other God.
⁷ Who is like me?
Let him step forward and prove to you his power.
Let him do as I have done since ancient times
when I established a people
and explained its future.
⁸ Do not tremble; do not be afraid.
Did I not proclaim my purposes for you long ago?
You are my witnesses—is there any other God?
No! There is no other Rock—not one!"
⁹ How foolish are those who manufacture idols.
These prized objects are really worthless.
The people who worship idols don't know this,
so they are all put to shame.
¹⁰ Who but a fool would make his own god—
an idol that cannot help him one bit?
¹¹ All who worship idols will be disgraced
along with all these craftsmen—mere humans—
who claim they can make a god.
They may all stand together,
but they will stand in terror and shame.
¹² The blacksmith stands at
his forge to make a sharp tool,
pounding and shaping it with all his might.
His work makes him hungry and weak.
It makes him thirsty and faint.
¹³ Then the wood-carver measures a block of wood
and draws a pattern on it.

He works with chisel and plane
and carves it into a human figure.
He gives it human beauty
and puts it in a little shrine.

[14] He cuts down cedars;
he selects the cypress and the oak;
he plants the pine in the forest
to be nourished by the rain.

[15] Then he uses part of the wood to make a fire.
With it he warms himself and bakes his bread.
Then—yes, it's true—he takes the rest of it
and makes himself a god to worship!
He makes an idol
and bows down in front of it!

[16] He burns part of the tree to roast his meat
and to keep himself warm.
He says, "Ah, that fire feels good."

[17] Then he takes what's left
and makes his god: a carved idol!
He falls down in front of it,
worshiping and praying to it.
"Rescue me!" he says.
"You are my god!"

[18] Such stupidity and ignorance!
Their eyes are closed, and they cannot see.
Their minds are shut, and they cannot think.

[19] The person who made the idol never stops to reflect,
"Why, it's just a block of wood!
I burned half of it for heat
and used it to bake my bread and roast my meat.
How can the rest of it be a god?
Should I bow down to worship a piece of wood?"

[20] The poor, deluded fool feeds on ashes.
He trusts something that can't help him at all.
Yet he cannot bring himself to ask,
"Is this idol that I'm holding in my hand a lie?"

RESTORATION FOR JERUSALEM

21 "Pay attention, O Jacob,
for you are my servant, O Israel.
I, the Lord, made you,
and I will not forget you.

22 I have swept away your sins like a cloud.
I have scattered your offenses
like the morning mist.
Oh, return to me,
for I have paid the price to set you free."

23 Sing, O heavens, for the Lord has
done this wondrous thing.
Shout for joy, O depths of the earth!
Break into song,
O mountains and forests and every tree!
For the Lord has redeemed Jacob
and is glorified in Israel.

24 This is what the Lord says—
your Redeemer and Creator:

"I am the Lord, who made all things.
I alone stretched out the heavens.
Who was with me
when I made the earth?

25 I expose the false prophets as liars
and make fools of fortune-tellers.
I cause the wise to give bad advice,
thus proving them to be fools.

26 But I carry out the predictions of my prophets!
By them I say to Jerusalem,
'People will live here again,'
and to the towns of Judah, 'You will be rebuilt;
I will restore all your ruins!'

27 When I speak to the rivers and say, 'Dry up!'
they will be dry.

28 When I say of Cyrus, 'He is my shepherd,'
he will certainly do as I say.
He will command, 'Rebuild Jerusalem';
he will say, 'Restore the Temple.'"

45

CYRUS, THE LORD'S CHOSEN ONE

1 This is what the Lord says
to Cyrus, his anointed one,
whose right hand he will empower.
Before him, mighty kings
will be paralyzed with fear.
Their fortress gates will be opened,
never to shut again.

2 This is what the Lord says:
"I will go before you, Cyrus,
and level the mountains.
I will smash down gates of bronze
and cut through bars of iron.

3 And I will give you treasures
hidden in the darkness—secret riches.
I will do this so you may know that I am the Lord,
the God of Israel, the one who calls you by name.

4 "And why have I called you for this work?
Why did I call you by name
when you did not know me?
It is for the sake of Jacob my servant,
Israel my chosen one.

5 I am the Lord; there is no other God.
I have equipped you for battle,
though you don't even know me,

6 so all the world from east to west
will know there is no other God.
I am the Lord, and there is no other.

7 I create the light and make the darkness.
I send good times and bad times.
I, the Lord, am the one who does these things.

8 "Open up, O heavens,
and pour out your righteousness.
Let the earth open wide
so salvation and righteousness
can sprout up together.
I, the Lord, created them.

9 "What sorrow awaits those who
argue with their Creator.
Does a clay pot argue with its maker?
Does the clay dispute with the one
who shapes it, saying,
'Stop, you're doing it wrong!'
Does the pot exclaim,
'How clumsy can you be?'

10 How terrible it would be if a newborn
baby said to its father,
'Why was I born?'
or if it said to its mother,
'Why did you make me this way?'"

11 This is what the Lord says—
the Holy One of Israel and your Creator:
"Do you question what I do for my children?
Do you give me orders
about the work of my hands?

12 I am the one who made the earth
and created people to live on it.
With my hands I stretched out the heavens.
All the stars are at my command.

13 I will raise up Cyrus
to fulfill my righteous purpose,
and I will guide his actions.
He will restore my city and
free my captive people—
without seeking a reward!
I, the Lord of Heaven's Armies, have spoken!"

FUTURE CONVERSION OF GENTILES

¹⁴ This is what the Lord says:

"You will rule the Egyptians,
the Ethiopians, and the Sabeans.
They will come to you with all their merchandise,
and it will all be yours.
They will follow you as prisoners in chains.
They will fall to their knees in front of you and say,
'God is with you, and he is the only God.
There is no other.'"

¹⁵ Truly, O God of Israel, our Savior,
you work in mysterious ways.

¹⁶ All craftsmen who make idols will be humiliated.
They will all be disgraced together.

¹⁷ But the Lord will save the people of Israel
with eternal salvation.
Throughout everlasting ages,
they will never again be humiliated and disgraced.

¹⁸ For the Lord is God,
and he created the heavens and earth
and put everything in place.
He made the world to be lived in,
not to be a place of empty chaos.
"I am the Lord," he says,
"and there is no other.

¹⁹ I publicly proclaim bold promises.
I do not whisper obscurities in some dark corner.
I would not have told
the people of Israel to seek me
if I could not be found.

I, the Lord, speak only what is true
and declare only what is right.

²⁰ "Gather together and come,
you fugitives from surrounding nations.
What fools they are who carry around
their wooden idols
and pray to gods that cannot save!

²¹ Consult together, argue your case.
Get together and decide what to say.
Who made these things known so long ago?
What idol ever told you they would happen?
Was it not I, the Lord?
For there is no other God but me,
a righteous God and Savior.
There is none but me.

²² Let all the world look to me for salvation!
For I am God; there is no other.

²³ I have sworn by my own name;
I have spoken the truth,
and I will never go back on my word:
Every knee will bend to me,
and every tongue will declare allegiance to me."

²⁴ The people will declare,
"The Lord is the source of all my
righteousness and strength."
And all who were angry with him
will come to him and be ashamed.

²⁵ In the Lord all the generations
of Israel will be justified,
and in him they will boast.

46

BABYLON'S FALSE GODS

1 Bel and Nebo, the gods of Babylon,
  bow as they are lowered to the ground.
  They are being hauled away on ox carts.
  The poor beasts stagger under the weight.
2 Both the idols and their owners are bowed down.
  The gods cannot protect the people,
  and the people cannot protect the gods.
  They go off into captivity together.
3 "Listen to me, descendants of Jacob,
  all you who remain in Israel.
  I have cared for you since you were born.
  Yes, I carried you before you were born.
4 I will be your God throughout your lifetime—
  until your hair is white with age.
  I made you, and I will care for you.
  I will carry you along and save you.
5 "To whom will you compare me?
  Who is my equal?
6 Some people pour out their silver and gold
  and hire a craftsman to make a god from it.
  Then they bow down and worship it!
7 They carry it around on their shoulders,
  and when they set it down, it stays there.

It can't even move!
And when someone prays to it, there is no answer.
It can't rescue anyone from trouble.
8 "Do not forget this! Keep it in mind!
Remember this, you guilty ones.
9 Remember the things I have done in the past.
For I alone am God!
I am God, and there is none like me.
10 Only I can tell you the future
before it even happens.
Everything I plan will come to pass,
for I do whatever I wish.
11 I will call a swift bird of prey from the east—
a leader from a distant land to come
and do my bidding.
I have said what I would do,
and I will do it.
12 "Listen to me, you stubborn people
who are so far from doing right.
13 For I am ready to set things right,
not in the distant future, but right now!
I am ready to save Jerusalem
and show my glory to Israel.

47

PREDICTION OF BABYLON'S FALL

¹ "Come down, virgin daughter of Babylon, and sit in the dust.
For your days of sitting on a throne have ended.
O daughter of Babylonia, never again will you be
the lovely princess, tender and delicate.
² Take heavy millstones and grind flour.
Remove your veil, and strip off your robe.
Expose yourself to public view.
³ You will be naked and burdened with shame.
I will take vengeance against you without pity."
⁴ Our Redeemer, whose name is the Lord of Heaven's Armies,
is the Holy One of Israel.
⁵ "O beautiful Babylon, sit now in darkness and silence.
Never again will you be known as the queen of kingdoms.
⁶ For I was angry with my chosen people
and punished them by letting them fall into your hands.
But you, Babylon, showed them no mercy.
You oppressed even the elderly.
⁷ You said, 'I will reign forever as queen of the world!'
You did not reflect on your actions
or think about their consequences.
⁸ "Listen to this, you pleasure-loving kingdom,
living at ease and feeling secure.

You say, 'I am the only one, and there is no other.
I will never be a widow or lose my children.'

9 Well, both these things will come upon you in a moment:
widowhood and the loss of your children.
Yes, these calamities will come upon you,
despite all your witchcraft and magic.

10 "You felt secure in your wickedness.
'No one sees me,' you said.
But your 'wisdom' and 'knowledge' have led you astray,
and you said, 'I am the only one, and there is no other.'

11 So disaster will overtake you,
and you won't be able to charm it away.
Calamity will fall upon you,
and you won't be able to buy your way out.
A catastrophe will strike you suddenly,
one for which you are not prepared.

12 "Now use your magical charms!
Use the spells you have worked at all these years!
Maybe they will do you some good.
Maybe they can make someone afraid of you.

13 All the advice you receive has made you tired.
Where are all your astrologers,
those stargazers who make predictions each month?
Let them stand up and save you
from what the future holds.

14 But they are like straw burning in a fire;
they cannot save themselves from the flame.
You will get no help from them at all;
their hearth is no place to sit for warmth.

15 And all your friends,
those with whom you've done business since childhood,
will go their own ways,
turning a deaf ear to your cries.

48

GOD'S STUBBORN PEOPLE

1 "Listen to me, O family of Jacob,
   you who are called by the name of Israel
   and born into the family of Judah.
   Listen, you who take oaths in the name of the Lord
   and call on the God of Israel.
   You don't keep your promises,
2 even though you call yourself the holy city
   and talk about depending on the God of Israel,
   whose name is the Lord of Heaven's Armies.
3 Long ago I told you what was going to happen.
   Then suddenly I took action,
   and all my predictions came true.
4 For I know how stubborn and obstinate you are.
   Your necks are as unbending as iron.
   Your heads are as hard as bronze.
5 That is why I told you what would happen;
   I told you beforehand what I was going to do.
   Then you could never say, 'My idols did it.
   My wooden image and

metal god commanded it to happen!'
6 You have heard my predictions
   and seen them fulfilled,
   but you refuse to admit it.
   Now I will tell you new things,
   secrets you have not yet heard.
7 They are brand new, not things from the past.
   So you cannot say, 'We knew that all the time!'
8 "Yes, I will tell you of things that are entirely new,
   things you never heard of before.
   For I know so well what traitors you are.
   You have been rebels from birth.
9 Yet for my own sake and for the honor of my name,
   I will hold back my anger and not wipe you out.
10 I have refined you, but not as silver is refined.
   Rather, I have refined you in the furnace of suffering.
11 I will rescue you for my sake—yes, for my own sake!
   I will not let my reputation be tarnished,
   and I will not share my glory with idols!

FREEDOM FROM BABYLON

¹² "Listen to me, O family of Jacob,
Israel my chosen one!
I alone am God,
the First and the Last.

¹³ It was my hand that laid
the foundations of the earth,
my right hand that spread out the heavens above.
When I call out the stars,
they all appear in order."

¹⁴ Have any of your idols ever told you this?
Come, all of you, and listen:
The Lord has chosen Cyrus as his ally.
He will use him to put an end to the empire of Babylon
and to destroy the Babylonian armies.

¹⁵ "I have said it: I am calling Cyrus!
I will send him on this errand
and will help him succeed.

¹⁶ Come closer, and listen to this.
From the beginning I have told you plainly what
would happen."
And now the Sovereign Lord and his Spirit
have sent me with this message.

¹⁷ This is what the Lord says—
your Redeemer, the Holy One of Israel:

"I am the Lord your God,
who teaches you what is good for you
and leads you along the paths you should follow.

¹⁸ Oh, that you had listened to my commands!
Then you would have had peace flowing
like a gentle river
and righteousness rolling over
you like waves in the sea.

¹⁹ Your descendants would have been like the sands
along the seashore—
too many to count!
There would have been no need for your destruction,
or for cutting off your family name."

²⁰ Yet even now, be free from your captivity!
Leave Babylon and the Babylonians.
Sing out this message!
Shout it to the ends of the earth!
The Lord has redeemed his servants,
the people of Israel.

²¹ They were not thirsty
when he led them through the desert.
He divided the rock,
and water gushed out for them to drink.

²² "But there is no peace for the wicked,"
says the Lord.

49

THE LORD'S SERVANT COMMISSIONED

¹ Listen to me, all you in distant lands!
Pay attention, you who are far away!
The Lord called me before my birth;
from within the womb he called me by name.

² He made my words of judgment as sharp as a sword.
He has hidden me in the shadow of his hand.
I am like a sharp arrow in his quiver.

³ He said to me, "You are my servant, Israel,
and you will bring me glory."

⁴ I replied, "But my work seems so useless!
I have spent my strength for nothing and to no purpose.
Yet I leave it all in the Lord's hand;
I will trust God for my reward."

⁵ And now the Lord speaks—
the one who formed me in my mother's womb to be his servant,
who commissioned me to bring Israel back to him.
The Lord has honored me,
and my God has given me strength.

⁶ He says, "You will do more than
restore the people of Israel to me.
I will make you a light to the Gentiles,
and you will bring my salvation to the ends of the earth."

⁷ The Lord, the Redeemer
and Holy One of Israel,
says to the one who is despised and rejected by the nations,
to the one who is the servant of rulers:
"Kings will stand at attention when you pass by.
Princes will also bow low
because of the Lord, the faithful one,
the Holy One of Israel, who has chosen you."

PROMISES OF ISRAEL'S RESTORATION

[8] This is what the Lord says:

"At just the right time, I will respond to you.

On the day of salvation I will help you.

I will protect you and give you to the people

as my covenant with them.

Through you I will reestablish the land of Israel

and assign it to its own people again.

[9] I will say to the prisoners, 'Come out in freedom,'

and to those in darkness, 'Come into the light.'

They will be my sheep, grazing in green pastures

and on hills that were previously bare.

[10] They will neither hunger nor thirst.

The searing sun will not reach them anymore.

For the Lord in his mercy will lead them;

he will lead them beside cool waters.

[11] And I will make my mountains

into level paths for them.

The highways will be raised above the valleys.

[12] See, my people will return from far away,

from lands to the north and west,

and from as far south as Egypt."

[13] Sing for joy, O heavens! Rejoice, O earth!

Burst into song, O mountains!

For the Lord has comforted his people

and will have compassion on them in their suffering.

[14] Yet Jerusalem says, "The Lord has deserted us;

the Lord has forgotten us."

[15] "Never! Can a mother forget her nursing child?

Can she feel no love for the child she has borne?

But even if that were possible,

I would not forget you!

[16] See, I have written your name

on the palms of my hands.

Always in my mind is a picture of

Jerusalem's walls in ruins.

[17] Soon your descendants will come back,

and all who are trying to destroy you will go away.

[18] Look around you and see,

for all your children will come back to you.

As surely as I live," says the Lord,

"they will be like jewels or

bridal ornaments for you to display.

[19] "Even the most desolate

parts of your abandoned land

will soon be crowded with your people.

Your enemies who enslaved you

will be far away.

[20] The generations born in exile will return and say,

'We need more room! It's crowded here!'

[21] Then you will think to yourself,

'Who has given me all these descendants?

For most of my children were killed,

and the rest were carried away into exile.

I was left here all alone.

Where did all these people come from?

Who bore these children?

Who raised them for me?'"

[22] This is what the Sovereign Lord says:

"See, I will give a signal to the godless nations.

They will carry your little sons

back to you in their arms;

they will bring your daughters on their shoulders.

[23] Kings and queens will serve you

and care for all your needs.

They will bow to the earth before you

and lick the dust from your feet.

Then you will know that I am the Lord.

Those who trust in me will never be put to shame."

[24] Who can snatch the plunder of war from the hands of a warrior?

Who can demand that a tyrant let his captives go?

[25] But the Lord says,

"The captives of warriors will be released,

and the plunder of tyrants will be retrieved.

For I will fight those who fight you,

and I will save your children.

[26] I will feed your enemies with their own flesh.

They will be drunk with rivers of their own blood.

All the world will know that I, the Lord,

am your Savior and your Redeemer,

the Mighty One of Israel."

50

1 This is what the Lord says:
"Was your mother sent
away because I divorced her?
Did I sell you as slaves to my creditors?
No, you were sold because of your sins.
And your mother, too,
was taken because of your sins.
2 Why was no one there when I came?
Why didn't anyone answer when I called?
Is it because I have no power to rescue?
No, that is not the reason!
For I can speak to the sea and make it dry up!
I can turn rivers into deserts
covered with dying fish.
3 I dress the skies in darkness,
covering them with clothes of mourning."

THE LORD'S OBEDIENT SERVANT

4 The Sovereign Lord has
given me his words of wisdom,
so that I know how to comfort the weary.
Morning by morning he wakens me
and opens my understanding to his will.
5 The Sovereign Lord has spoken to me,
and I have listened.
I have not rebelled or turned away.

6 I offered my back to those who beat me
and my cheeks to those who pulled out my beard.
I did not hide my face
from mockery and spitting.
7 Because the Sovereign Lord helps me,
I will not be disgraced.
Therefore, I have set my face like a stone,
determined to do his will.
And I know that I will not be put to shame.
8 He who gives me justice is near.
Who will dare to bring charges against me now?
Where are my accusers?
Let them appear!
9 See, the Sovereign Lord is on my side!
Who will declare me guilty?
All my enemies will be destroyed
like old clothes that have been eaten by moths!
10 Who among you fears the Lord
and obeys his servant?
If you are walking in darkness,
without a ray of light,
trust in the Lord and rely on your God.
11 But watch out, you who live in your own light
and warm yourselves by your own fires.
This is the reward you will receive from me:
You will soon fall down in great torment.

51

A CALL TO TRUST THE LORD

1 "Listen to me, all who hope for deliverance—
all who seek the Lord!
Consider the rock from which you were cut,
the quarry from which you were mined.

2 Yes, think about Abraham, your ancestor,
and Sarah, who gave birth to your nation.
Abraham was only one man when I called him.
But when I blessed him, he became a great nation."

3 The Lord will comfort Israel again
and have pity on her ruins.
Her desert will blossom like Eden,
her barren wilderness like the garden of the Lord.
Joy and gladness will be found there.
Songs of thanksgiving will fill the air.

4 "Listen to me, my people.
Hear me, Israel, for my law will be proclaimed,
and my justice will become a light to the nations.

5 My mercy and justice are coming soon.
My salvation is on the way.
My strong arm will bring justice to the nations.
All distant lands will look to me
and wait in hope for my powerful arm.

6 Look up to the skies above,
and gaze down on the earth below.
For the skies will disappear like smoke,
and the earth will wear out like a piece of clothing.

The people of the earth will die like flies,
but my salvation lasts forever.
My righteous rule will never end!

7 "Listen to me, you who know right from wrong,
you who cherish my law in your hearts.
Do not be afraid of people's scorn,
nor fear their insults.

8 For the moth will devour them as it devours clothing.
The worm will eat at them as it eats wool.
But my righteousness will last forever.
My salvation will continue
from generation to generation."

9 Wake up, wake up, O Lord!
Clothe yourself with strength!
Flex your mighty right arm!
Rouse yourself as in the days of old
when you slew Egypt, the dragon of the Nile.

10 Are you not the same today,
the one who dried up the sea,
making a path of escape through the depths
so that your people could cross over?

11 Those who have been ransomed
by the Lord will return.
They will enter Jerusalem singing,
crowned with everlasting joy.
Sorrow and mourning will disappear,
and they will be filled with joy and gladness.

[12] "I, yes I, am the one who comforts you.
So why are you afraid of mere humans,
who wither like the grass and disappear?

[13] Yet you have forgotten the Lord, your Creator,
the one who stretched out the sky like a canopy
and laid the foundations of the earth.
Will you remain in constant
dread of human oppressors?
Will you continue to fear the anger of your enemies?
Where is their fury and anger now?
It is gone!

[14] Soon all you captives will be released!
Imprisonment, starvation,
and death will not be your fate!

[15] For I am the Lord your God,
who stirs up the sea, causing its waves to roar.
My name is the Lord of Heaven's Armies.

[16] And I have put my words in your mouth
and hidden you safely in my hand.
I stretched out the sky like a canopy
and laid the foundations of the earth.
I am the one who says to Israel,
'You are my people!'"

[17] Wake up, wake up, O Jerusalem!
You have drunk the cup of the Lord's fury.
You have drunk the cup of terror,
tipping out its last drops.

[18] Not one of your children is left alive
to take your hand and guide you.

[19] These two calamities have fallen on you:
desolation and destruction, famine and war.
And who is left to sympathize with you?
Who is left to comfort you?

[20] For your children have fainted and lie in the streets,
helpless as antelopes caught in a net.
The Lord has poured out his fury;
God has rebuked them.

[21] But now listen to this, you afflicted ones
who sit in a drunken stupor,
though not from drinking wine.

[22] This is what the Sovereign Lord,
your God and Defender, says:
"See, I have taken the terrible
cup from your hands.
You will drink no more of my fury.

[23] Instead, I will hand that cup to your tormentors,
those who said, 'We will trample you into the dust
and walk on your backs.'"

52

DELIVERANCE FOR JERUSALEM

1 "Wake up, wake up, O Zion!
  Clothe yourself with strength.
  Put on your beautiful clothes,
  O holy city of Jerusalem,
  for unclean and godless people will enter
  your gates no longer.

2 Rise from the dust, O Jerusalem.
  Sit in a place of honor.
  Remove the chains of slavery from your neck,
  O captive daughter of Zion.

3 For this is what the Lord says:
  "When I sold you into exile,
  I received no payment.
  Now I can redeem you
  without having to pay for you."

4 This is what the Sovereign Lord says: "Long ago my people chose to live in Egypt. Now they are oppressed by Assyria. 5 What is this?" asks the Lord. "Why are my people enslaved again? Those who rule them shout in exultation. My name is blasphemed all day long. 6 But I will reveal my name to my people, and they will come to know its power. Then at last they will recognize that I am the one who speaks to them."

7 How beautiful on the mountains
  are the feet of the messenger who brings good news,
  the good news of peace and salvation,
  the news that the God of Israel reigns!

8 The watchmen shout and sing with joy,
  for before their very eyes
  they see the Lord returning to Jerusalem.

9 Let the ruins of Jerusalem break into joyful song,
  for the Lord has comforted his people.
  He has redeemed Jerusalem.

10 The Lord has demonstrated his holy power
  before the eyes of all the nations.
  All the ends of the earth will see
  the victory of our God.

11 Get out! Get out and leave your captivity,
  where everything you touch is unclean.
  Get out of there and purify yourselves,
  you who carry home the sacred objects of the Lord.

12 You will not leave in a hurry,
  running for your lives.
  For the Lord will go ahead of you;
  yes, the God of Israel will protect you from behind.

THE LORD'S SUFFERING SERVANT

13 See, my servant will prosper;
  he will be highly exalted.

14 But many were amazed when they saw him.
  His face was so disfigured
  he seemed hardly human,
  and from his appearance, one would scarcely
  know he was a man.

15 And he will startle many nations.
  Kings will stand speechless in his presence.
  For they will see what they had not been told;
  they will understand
  what they had not heard about.

53

[1] Who has believed our message?
To whom has the Lord revealed his powerful arm?

[2] My servant grew up in the Lord's
presence like a tender green shoot,
like a root in dry ground.
There was nothing beautiful or majestic about his appearance,
nothing to attract us to him.

[3] He was despised and rejected—
a man of sorrows, acquainted with deepest grief.
We turned our backs on him and looked the other way.
He was despised, and we did not care.

[4] Yet it was our weaknesses he carried;
it was our sorrows that weighed him down.
And we thought his troubles were a punishment from God,
a punishment for his own sins!

[5] But he was pierced for our rebellion,
crushed for our sins.
He was beaten so we could be whole.
He was whipped so we could be healed.

[6] All of us, like sheep, have strayed away.
We have left God's paths to follow our own.
Yet the Lord laid on him
the sins of us all.

⁷ He was oppressed and treated harshly,
yet he never said a word.
He was led like a lamb to the slaughter.
And as a sheep is silent before the shearers,
he did not open his mouth.
⁸ Unjustly condemned,
he was led away.
No one cared that he died without descendants,
that his life was cut short in midstream.
But he was struck down
for the rebellion of my people.
⁹ He had done no wrong
and had never deceived anyone.
But he was buried like a criminal;
he was put in a rich man's grave.
¹⁰ But it was the Lord's good plan to crush him
and cause him grief.
Yet when his life is made an offering for sin,
he will have many descendants.
He will enjoy a long life,
and the Lord's good plan will prosper in his hands.
¹¹ When he sees all that is accomplished by his anguish,
he will be satisfied.
And because of his experience,
my righteous servant will make it possible
for many to be counted righteous,
for he will bear all their sins.
¹² I will give him the honors of a victorious soldier,
because he exposed himself to death.
He was counted among the rebels.
He bore the sins of many and interceded for rebels.

54

FUTURE GLORY FOR JERUSALEM

1 "Sing, O childless woman,
you who have never given birth!
Break into loud and joyful song, O Jerusalem,
you who have never been in labor.
For the desolate woman now has more children
than the woman who lives with her husband,"
says the Lord.

2 "Enlarge your house; build an addition.
Spread out your home, and spare no expense!

3 For you will soon be bursting at the seams.
Your descendants will occupy other nations
and resettle the ruined cities.

4 "Fear not; you will no longer live in shame.
Don't be afraid; there is no more disgrace for you.
You will no longer remember the shame
of your youth and the sorrows of widowhood.

5 For your Creator will be your husband;
the Lord of Heaven's Armies is his name!
He is your Redeemer, the Holy One of Israel,
the God of all the earth.

6 For the Lord has called you back from your grief—
as though you were a young wife abandoned by
her husband," says your God.

7 "For a brief moment I abandoned you,
but with great compassion I will take you back.

8 In a burst of anger I turned my face
away for a little while.
But with everlasting love I will have
compassion on you,"
says the Lord, your Redeemer.

9 "Just as I swore in the time of Noah
that I would never again let a
flood cover the earth, so now I swear
that I will never again be angry and punish you.

10 For the mountains may move
and the hills disappear,
but even then my faithful love for you will remain.
My covenant of blessing will never be broken,"
says the Lord, who has mercy on you.

11 "O storm-battered city,
troubled and desolate!

I will rebuild you with precious jewels
and make your foundations from lapis lazuli.

[12] I will make your towers of sparkling rubies,
your gates of shining gems,
and your walls of precious stones.

[13] I will teach all your children,
and they will enjoy great peace.

[14] You will be secure under a government that is just and fair.
Your enemies will stay far away.
You will live in peace,
and terror will not come near.

[15] If any nation comes to fight you,
it is not because I sent them.
Whoever attacks you will go down in defeat.

[16] "I have created the blacksmith
who fans the coals beneath the forge
and makes the weapons of destruction.
And I have created the armies that destroy.

[17] But in that coming day
no weapon turned against you will succeed.
You will silence every voice
raised up to accuse you.
These benefits are enjoyed by the servants of the Lord;
their vindication will come from me.
I, the Lord, have spoken!

55

INVITATION TO THE LORD'S SALVATION

1 "Is anyone thirsty?
Come and drink—
even if you have no money!
Come, take your choice of wine or milk—
it's all free!

2 Why spend your money on food that does not give
you strength?
Why pay for food that does you no good?
Listen to me, and you will eat what is good.
You will enjoy the finest food.

3 "Come to me with your ears wide open.
Listen, and you will find life.
I will make an everlasting covenant with you.
I will give you all the unfailing
love I promised to David.

4 See how I used him to display
my power among the peoples.
I made him a leader among the nations.

5 You also will command
nations you do not know,
and peoples unknown to you
will come running to obey,
because I, the Lord your God,
the Holy One of Israel, have made you glorious."

6 Seek the Lord while you can find him.
Call on him now while he is near.

7 Let the wicked change their ways
and banish the very thought of doing wrong.

Let them turn to the Lord
that he may have mercy on them.
Yes, turn to our God, for he will forgive generously.

8 "My thoughts are nothing like your thoughts,"
says the Lord.
"And my ways are far beyond
anything you could imagine.

9 For just as the heavens are higher than the earth,
so my ways are higher than your ways
and my thoughts higher than your thoughts.

10 "The rain and snow come down from the heavens
and stay on the ground to water the earth.
They cause the grain to grow,
producing seed for the farmer
and bread for the hungry.

11 It is the same with my word.
I send it out, and it always produces fruit.
It will accomplish all I want it to,
and it will prosper everywhere I send it.

12 You will live in joy and peace.
The mountains and hills will burst into song,
and the trees of the field will clap their hands!

13 Where once there were thorns,
cypress trees will grow.
Where nettles grew, myrtles will sprout up.
These events will bring great
honor to the Lord's name;
they will be an everlasting
sign of his power and love."

56

BLESSINGS FOR ALL NATIONS

1 This is what the Lord says:
"Be just and fair to all.
Do what is right and good,
for I am coming soon to rescue you
and to display my righteousness among you.

2 Blessed are all those
who are careful to do this.
Blessed are those who
honor my Sabbath days of rest
and keep themselves from doing wrong.

3 "Don't let foreigners who commit themselves to
the Lord say,
'The Lord will never let me be part of his people.'
And don't let the eunuchs say,
'I'm a dried-up tree with
no children and no future.'

4 For this is what the Lord says:
I will bless those eunuchs
who keep my Sabbath days holy
and who choose to do what pleases me
and commit their lives to me.

5 I will give them—within the walls of my house—
a memorial and a name
far greater than sons and daughters could give.
For the name I give them is an everlasting one.
It will never disappear!

6 "I will also bless the foreigners who commit
themselves to the Lord,
who serve him and love his name,
who worship him and do not
desecrate the Sabbath day of rest,

and who hold fast to my covenant.

7 I will bring them to my
holy mountain of Jerusalem
and will fill them with joy
in my house of prayer.
I will accept their burnt offerings and sacrifices,
because my Temple will be called
a house of prayer for all nations.

8 For the Sovereign Lord,
who brings back the outcasts of Israel, says:
I will bring others, too,
besides my people Israel."

SINFUL LEADERS CONDEMNED

9 Come, wild animals of the field!
Come, wild animals of the forest!
Come and devour my people!

10 For the leaders of my people—
the Lord's watchmen, his shepherds—
are blind and ignorant.
They are like silent watchdogs
that give no warning when danger comes.
They love to lie around, sleeping and dreaming.

11 Like greedy dogs, they are never satisfied.
They are ignorant shepherds,
all following their own path
and intent on personal gain.

12 "Come," they say, "let's get
some wine and have a party.
Let's all get drunk.
Then tomorrow we'll do it again
and have an even bigger party!"

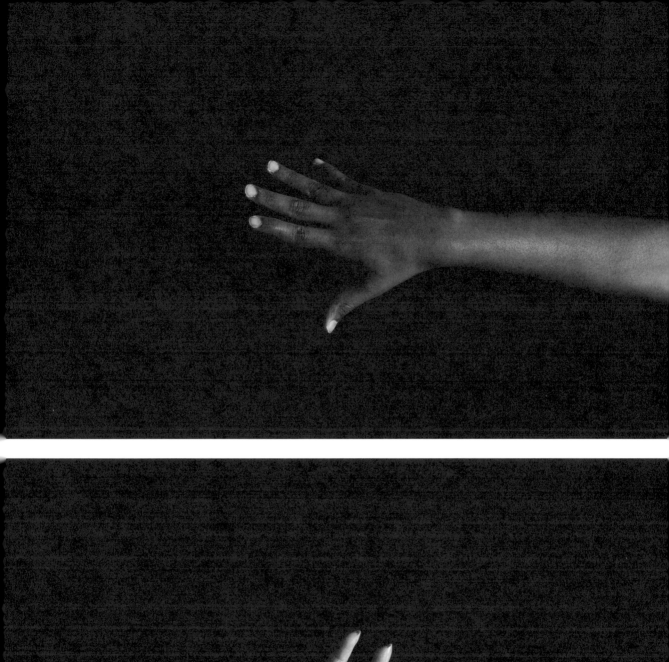

57

¹ Good people pass away;
  the godly often die before their time.
  But no one seems to care or wonder why.
  No one seems to understand
  that God is protecting them from the evil to come.
² For those who follow godly paths
  will rest in peace when they die.

IDOLATROUS WORSHIP CONDEMNED

³ "But you—come here, you witches' children,
  you offspring of adulterers and prostitutes!
⁴ Whom do you mock,
  making faces and sticking out your tongues?
  You children of sinners and liars!
⁵ You worship your idols with great passion
  beneath the oaks and under every green tree.
  You sacrifice your children down in the valleys,
  among the jagged rocks in the cliffs.
⁶ Your gods are the smooth stones in the valleys.
  You worship them with liquid offerings
  and grain offerings.
  They, not I, are your inheritance.
  Do you think all this makes me happy?
⁷ You have committed adultery
  on every high mountain.
  There you have worshiped idols
  and have been unfaithful to me.
⁸ You have put pagan symbols
  on your doorposts and behind your doors.
  You have left me
  and climbed into bed with these detestable gods.
  You have committed yourselves to them.
  You love to look at their naked bodies.
⁹ You have gone to Molech
  with olive oil and many perfumes,
  sending your agents far and wide,
  even to the world of the dead.
¹⁰ You grew weary in your search,
  but you never gave up.
  Desire gave you renewed strength,
  and you did not grow weary.
¹¹ "Are you afraid of these idols?
  Do they terrify you?
  Is that why you have lied to me
  and forgotten me and my words?
  Is it because of my long silence
  that you no longer fear me?
¹² Now I will expose your
  so-called good deeds.
  None of them will help you.
¹³ Let's see if your idols can save you
  when you cry to them for help.
  Why, a puff of wind can knock them down!
  If you just breathe on them, they fall over!
  But whoever trusts in me will inherit the land
  and possess my holy mountain."

GOD FORGIVES THE REPENTANT

¹⁴ God says, "Rebuild the road!
Clear away the rocks and stones
so my people can return from captivity."

¹⁵ The high and lofty one who lives in eternity,
the Holy One, says this:
"I live in the high and holy place
with those whose spirits are contrite and humble.
I restore the crushed spirit of the humble
and revive the courage of those with repentant hearts.

¹⁶ For I will not fight against you forever;
I will not always be angry.
If I were, all people would pass away—
all the souls I have made.

¹⁷ I was angry,
so I punished these greedy people.
I withdrew from them,
but they kept going on their own stubborn way.

¹⁸ I have seen what they do,
but I will heal them anyway!
I will lead them.
I will comfort those who mourn,

¹⁹ bringing words of praise to their lips.
May they have abundant peace, both near and far,"
says the Lord, who heals them.

²⁰ "But those who still reject me are like the restless sea,
which is never still
but continually churns up mud and dirt.

²¹ There is no peace for the wicked,"
says my God.

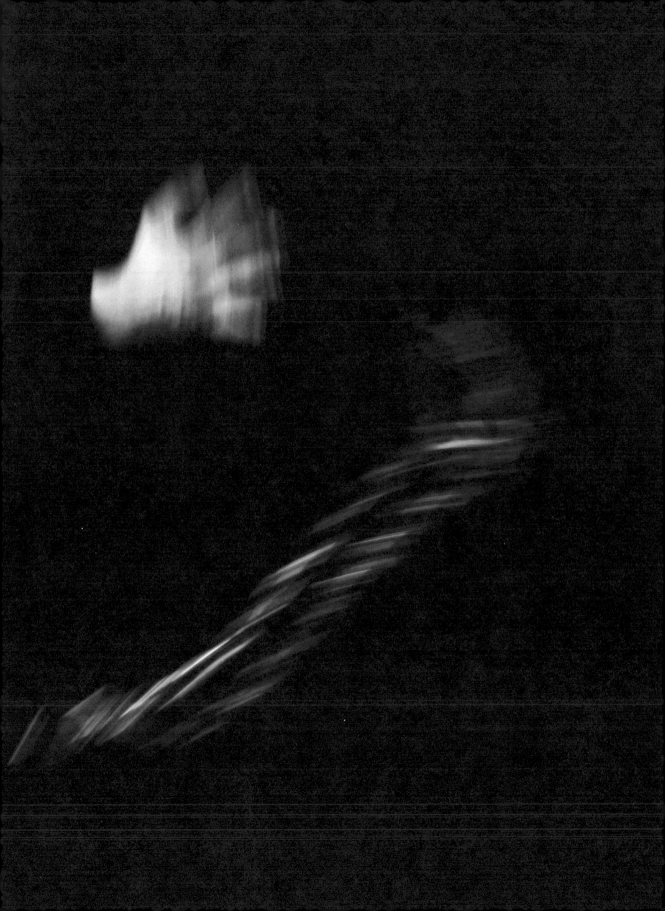

58

TRUE AND FALSE WORSHIP

1 "Shout with the voice of a trumpet blast.
Shout aloud! Don't be timid.
Tell my people Israel of their sins!

2 Yet they act so pious!
They come to the Temple every day
and seem delighted to learn all about me.
They act like a righteous nation
that would never abandon the laws of its God.
They ask me to take action on their behalf,
pretending they want to be near me.

3 'We have fasted before you!' they say.
'Why aren't you impressed?
We have been very hard on ourselves,
and you don't even notice it!'
"I will tell you why!" I respond.
"It's because you are fasting to please yourselves.
Even while you fast,
you keep oppressing your workers.

4 What good is fasting
when you keep on fighting and quarreling?
This kind of fasting
will never get you anywhere with me.

5 You humble yourselves
by going through the motions of penance,
bowing your heads
like reeds bending in the wind.
You dress in burlap
and cover yourselves with ashes.
Is this what you call fasting?
Do you really think this will please the Lord?

6 "No, this is the kind of fasting I want:
Free those who are wrongly imprisoned;
lighten the burden of those who work for you.
Let the oppressed go free,
and remove the chains that bind people.

7 Share your food with the hungry,
and give shelter to the homeless.
Give clothes to those who need them,
and do not hide from relatives who need your help.

8 "Then your salvation will come like the dawn,
and your wounds will quickly heal.
Your godliness will lead you forward,
and the glory of the Lord
will protect you from behind.

9 Then when you call, the Lord will answer.
'Yes, I am here,' he will quickly reply.
"Remove the heavy yoke of oppression.
Stop pointing your finger
and spreading vicious rumors!

¹⁰ Feed the hungry,

and help those in trouble.

Then your light will shine out from the darkness,

and the darkness around you will be as bright as noon.

¹¹ The Lord will guide you continually,

giving you water when you are dry

and restoring your strength.

You will be like a well-watered garden,

like an ever-flowing spring.

¹² Some of you will rebuild the deserted ruins of your cities.

Then you will be known as a rebuilder of walls

and a restorer of homes.

¹³ "Keep the Sabbath day holy.

Don't pursue your own interests on that day,

but enjoy the Sabbath

and speak of it with delight as the Lord's holy day.

Honor the Sabbath in everything you do on that day,

and don't follow your own desires or talk idly.

¹⁴ Then the Lord will be your delight.

I will give you great honor

and satisfy you with the inheritance

I promised to your ancestor Jacob.

I, the Lord, have spoken!"

59

WARNINGS AGAINST SIN

¹ Listen! The Lord's arm is not too weak to save you,
nor is his ear too deaf to hear you call.

² It's your sins that have cut you off from God.
Because of your sins, he has turned away
and will not listen anymore.

³ Your hands are the hands of murderers,
and your fingers are filthy with sin.
Your lips are full of lies,
and your mouth spews corruption.

⁴ No one cares about being fair and honest.
The people's lawsuits are based on lies.
They conceive evil deeds
and then give birth to sin.

⁵ They hatch deadly snakes
and weave spiders' webs.
Whoever eats their eggs will die;
whoever cracks them will hatch a viper.

⁶ Their webs can't be made into clothing,
and nothing they do is productive.
All their activity is filled with sin,
and violence is their trademark.

⁷ Their feet run to do evil,
and they rush to commit murder.
They think only about sinning.
Misery and destruction always follow them.

⁸ They don't know where to find peace
or what it means to be just and good.

They have mapped out crooked roads,
and no one who follows them
knows a moment's peace.

⁹ So there is no justice among us,
and we know nothing about right living.
We look for light but find only darkness.
We look for bright skies but walk in gloom.

¹⁰ We grope like the blind along a wall,
feeling our way like people without eyes.
Even at brightest noontime,
we stumble as though it were dark.
Among the living,
we are like the dead.

¹¹ We growl like hungry bears;
we moan like mournful doves.
We look for justice, but it never comes.
We look for rescue, but it is far away from us.

¹² For our sins are piled up before God
and testify against us.
Yes, we know what sinners we are.

¹³ We know we have rebelled and have denied the Lord.
We have turned our backs on our God.
We know how unfair and oppressive we have been,
carefully planning our deceitful lies.

¹⁴ Our courts oppose the righteous,
and justice is nowhere to be found.
Truth stumbles in the streets,
and honesty has been outlawed.

¹⁵ Yes, truth is gone,

and anyone who renounces evil is attacked.

The Lord looked and was displeased

to find there was no justice.

¹⁶ He was amazed to see that no one intervened

to help the oppressed.

So he himself stepped in to save them

with his strong arm,

and his justice sustained him.

¹⁷ He put on righteousness as his body armor

and placed the helmet of salvation on his head.

He clothed himself with a robe of vengeance

and wrapped himself in a cloak of divine passion.

¹⁸ He will repay his enemies for their evil deeds.

His fury will fall on his foes.

He will pay them back even to the ends of the earth.

¹⁹ In the west, people will respect the name of the Lord;

in the east, they will glorify him.

For he will come like a raging flood tide

driven by the breath of the Lord.

²⁰ "The Redeemer will come to Jerusalem

to buy back those in Israel

who have turned from their sins,"

says the Lord.

²¹ "And this is my covenant with them," says the Lord. "My Spirit will not leave them, and neither will these words I have given you. They will be on your lips and on the lips of your children and your children's children forever. I, the Lord, have spoken!

60

FUTURE GLORY FOR JERUSALEM

1 "Arise, Jerusalem! Let your light shine for all to see.
For the glory of the Lord rises to shine on you.

2 Darkness as black as night covers all the nations
of the earth,
but the glory of the Lord rises and appears over you.

3 All nations will come to your light;
mighty kings will come to see your radiance.

4 "Look and see, for everyone is coming home!
Your sons are coming from distant lands;
your little daughters will be carried home.

5 Your eyes will shine,
and your heart will thrill with joy,
for merchants from around
the world will come to you.
They will bring you the wealth of many lands.

6 Vast caravans of camels will converge on you,
the camels of Midian and Ephah.
The people of Sheba will
bring gold and frankincense
and will come worshiping the Lord.

7 The flocks of Kedar will be given to you,
and the rams of Nebaioth
will be brought for my altars.

I will accept their offerings,
and I will make my Temple glorious.

8 "And what do I see flying like clouds to Israel,
like doves to their nests?

9 They are ships from the ends of the earth,
from lands that trust in me,
led by the great ships of Tarshish.
They are bringing the people of
Israel home from far away,
carrying their silver and gold.
They will honor the Lord your God,
the Holy One of Israel,
for he has filled you with splendor.

10 "Foreigners will come to rebuild your towns,
and their kings will serve you.
For though I have destroyed you in my anger,
I will now have mercy on you through my grace.

11 Your gates will stay open day and night
to receive the wealth of many lands. The kings
of the world will be led as
captives in a victory procession.

12 For the nations that refuse to serve you
will be destroyed.

¹³ "The glory of Lebanon will be yours—
the forests of cypress, fir, and pine—
to beautify my sanctuary.
My Temple will be glorious!

¹⁴ The descendants of your tormentors
will come and bow before you.
Those who despised you
will kiss your feet.
They will call you the City of the Lord,
and Zion of the Holy One of Israel.

¹⁵ "Though you were once despised and hated,
with no one traveling through you,
I will make you beautiful forever,
a joy to all generations.

¹⁶ Powerful kings and mighty nations
will satisfy your every need,
as though you were a child
nursing at the breast of a queen.
You will know at last that I, the Lord,
am your Savior and your Redeemer,
the Mighty One of Israel.

¹⁷ I will exchange your bronze for gold,
your iron for silver,
your wood for bronze,
and your stones for iron.

I will make peace your leader
and righteousness your ruler.

¹⁸ Violence will disappear from your land;
the desolation and destruction of war will end.
Salvation will surround you like city walls,
and praise will be on the lips of all who enter there.

¹⁹ "No longer will you need the sun to shine by day,
nor the moon to give its light by night,
for the Lord your God will
be your everlasting light,
and your God will be your glory.

²⁰ Your sun will never set;
your moon will not go down.
For the Lord will be your everlasting light.
Your days of mourning will come to an end.

²¹ All your people will be righteous.
They will possess their land forever,
for I will plant them there with my own hands
in order to bring myself glory.

²² The smallest family will
become a thousand people,
and the tiniest group will
become a mighty nation.
At the right time, I, the Lord,
will make it happen."

61

GOOD NEWS FOR THE OPPRESSED

1 The Spirit of the Sovereign Lord is upon me,
for the Lord has anointed me
to bring good news to the poor.
He has sent me to comfort the brokenhearted
and to proclaim that captives will be released
and prisoners will be freed.

2 He has sent me to tell those who mourn
that the time of the Lord's favor has come,
and with it, the day of God's anger
against their enemies.

3 To all who mourn in Israel,
he will give a crown of beauty for ashes,
a joyous blessing instead of mourning,
festive praise instead of despair.
In their righteousness, they will be like great oaks
that the Lord has planted for his own glory.

4 They will rebuild the ancient ruins,
repairing cities destroyed long ago.
They will revive them,
though they have been
deserted for many generations.

5 Foreigners will be your servants.
They will feed your flocks and plow your fields
and tend your vineyards.

6 You will be called priests of the Lord,
ministers of our God.

You will feed on the treasures of the nations
and boast in their riches.

7 Instead of shame and dishonor,
you will enjoy a double share of honor.
You will possess a double portion of
prosperity in your land,
and everlasting joy will be yours.

8 "For I, the Lord, love justice.
I hate robbery and wrongdoing.
I will faithfully reward my people for their suffering
and make an everlasting covenant with them.

9 Their descendants will be recognized
and honored among the nations.
Everyone will realize that they are a people
the Lord has blessed."

10 I am overwhelmed with joy in the Lord my God!
For he has dressed me with the clothing of salvation
and draped me in a robe of righteousness.
I am like a bridegroom dressed for his wedding
or a bride with her jewels.

11 The Sovereign Lord will show his justice to the
nations of the world.
Everyone will praise him!
His righteousness will be
like a garden in early spring,
with plants springing up everywhere.

62

ISAIAH'S PRAYER FOR JERUSALEM

¹ Because I love Zion,
I will not keep still.
Because my heart yearns for Jerusalem,
I cannot remain silent.
I will not stop praying for her
until her righteousness shines like the dawn,
and her salvation blazes like a burning torch.

² The nations will see your righteousness.
World leaders will be blinded by your glory.
And you will be given a new name
by the Lord's own mouth.

³ The Lord will hold you in his hand for all to see—
a splendid crown in the hand of God.

⁴ Never again will you be called "The Forsaken City"
or "The Desolate Land."
Your new name will be "The City of God's Delight"
and "The Bride of God,"
for the Lord delights in you
and will claim you as his bride.

⁵ Your children will commit themselves to you, O Jerusalem,
just as a young man commits himself to his bride.
Then God will rejoice over you
as a bridegroom rejoices over his bride.

6 O Jerusalem, I have posted
watchmen on your walls;
they will pray day and night, continually.
Take no rest, all you who pray to the Lord.

7 Give the Lord no rest until he completes his work,
until he makes Jerusalem the pride of the earth.

8 The Lord has sworn to
Jerusalem by his own strength:
"I will never again hand you over to your enemies.
Never again will foreign warriors come
and take away your grain and new wine.

9 You raised the grain, and you will eat it,
praising the Lord.
Within the courtyards of the Temple,
you yourselves will drink
the wine you have pressed."

10 Go out through the gates!
Prepare the highway for my people to return!
Smooth out the road; pull out the boulders;
raise a flag for all the nations to see.

11 The Lord has sent this message to every land:
"Tell the people of Israel,
'Look, your Savior is coming.
See, he brings his reward with him as he comes.'"

12 They will be called "The Holy People"
and "The People Redeemed by the Lord."
And Jerusalem will be known as
"The Desirable Place"
and "The City No Longer Forsaken."

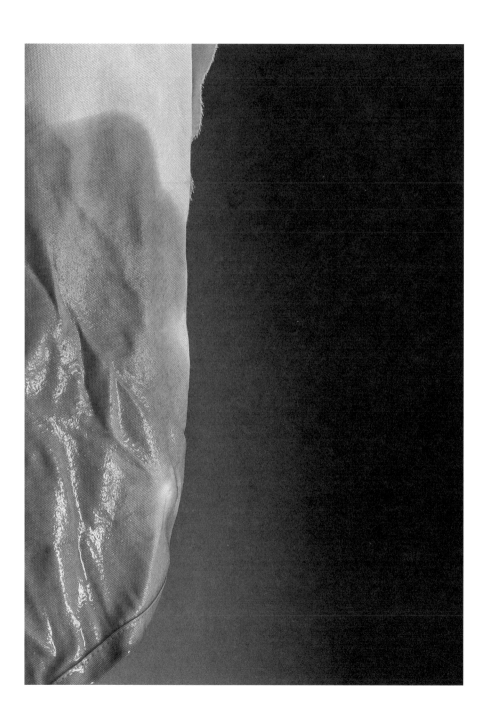

63

JUDGMENT AGAINST THE LORD'S ENEMIES

¹ Who is this who comes from Edom,
from the city of Bozrah,
with his clothing stained red?
Who is this in royal robes,
marching in his great strength?
"It is I, the Lord, announcing your salvation!
It is I, the Lord, who has the power to save!"

² Why are your clothes so red,
as if you have been treading out grapes?

³ "I have been treading the winepress alone;
no one was there to help me.
In my anger I have trampled my enemies
as if they were grapes.
In my fury I have trampled my foes.
Their blood has stained my clothes.

⁴ For the time has come for me to avenge my people,
to ransom them from their oppressors.

⁵ I was amazed to see that no one intervened
to help the oppressed.
So I myself stepped in to save
them with my strong arm,
and my wrath sustained me.

⁶ I crushed the nations in my anger
and made them stagger and fall to the ground,
spilling their blood upon the earth."

PRAISE FOR DELIVERANCE

7 I will tell of the Lord's unfailing love.
I will praise the Lord for all he has done.
I will rejoice in his great goodness to Israel,
which he has granted
according to his mercy and love.

8 He said, "They are my very own people.
Surely they will not betray me again."
And he became their Savior.

9 In all their suffering he also suffered,
and he personally rescued them.
In his love and mercy he redeemed them.
He lifted them up and carried them
through all the years.

10 But they rebelled against him
and grieved his Holy Spirit.
So he became their enemy
and fought against them.

11 Then they remembered those days of old
when Moses led his people out of Egypt.
They cried out, "Where is the one who brought
Israel through the sea,
with Moses as their shepherd?
Where is the one who sent his Holy Spirit
to be among his people?

12 Where is the one whose power was displayed
when Moses lifted up his hand—
the one who divided the sea before them,
making himself famous forever?

13 Where is the one who led them through the bottom
of the sea?

They were like fine stallions
racing through the desert, never stumbling.

14 As with cattle going down into a peaceful valley,
the Spirit of the Lord gave them rest.
You led your people, Lord,
and gained a magnificent reputation."

PRAYER FOR MERCY AND PARDON

15 Lord, look down from heaven;
look from your holy, glorious home, and see us.
Where is the passion and the might
you used to show on our behalf?
Where are your mercy and compassion now?

16 Surely you are still our Father!
Even if Abraham and Jacob would disown us,
Lord, you would still be our Father.
You are our Redeemer from ages past.

17 Lord, why have you allowed
us to turn from your path?
Why have you given us
stubborn hearts so
we no longer fear you?
Return and help us, for we are your servants,
the tribes that are your special possession.

18 How briefly your holy people
possessed your holy place,
and now our enemies have destroyed it.

19 Sometimes it seems as though
we never belonged to you,
as though we had never been
known as your people.

64

¹ Oh, that you would burst from
the heavens and come down!
How the mountains would quake in your presence!
² As fire causes wood to burn
and water to boil,
your coming would make the nations tremble.
Then your enemies would learn
the reason for your fame!
³ When you came down long ago, you did awesome
deeds beyond our highest expectations.
And oh, how the mountains quaked!
⁴ For since the world began,
no ear has heard
and no eye has seen a God like you,
who works for those who wait for him!
⁵ You welcome those who gladly do good,
who follow godly ways.
But you have been very angry with us,
for we are not godly.
We are constant sinners;
how can people like us be saved?
⁶ We are all infected and impure with sin.
When we display our righteous deeds,

they are nothing but filthy rags.
Like autumn leaves, we wither and fall,
and our sins sweep us away like the wind.
⁷ Yet no one calls on your name
or pleads with you for mercy.
Therefore, you have turned away from us
and turned us over to our sins.
⁸ And yet, O Lord, you are our Father.
We are the clay, and you are the potter.
We all are formed by your hand.
⁹ Don't be so angry with us, Lord.
Please don't remember our sins forever.
Look at us, we pray,
and see that we are all your people.
¹⁰ Your holy cities are destroyed.
Zion is a wilderness;
yes, Jerusalem is a desolate ruin.
¹¹ The holy and beautiful Temple
where our ancestors praised you
has been burned down,
and all the things of beauty are destroyed.
¹² After all this, Lord, must you still refuse to help us?
Will you continue to be silent and punish us?

65

JUDGMENT AND FINAL SALVATION

1 The Lord says,
"I was ready to respond, but no one asked for help.
I was ready to be found,
but no one was looking for me.
I said, 'Here I am, here I am!'
to a nation that did not call on my name.

2 All day long I opened my arms
to a rebellious people.
But they follow their own evil paths
and their own crooked schemes.

3 All day long they insult me to my face
by worshiping idols in their sacred gardens.
They burn incense on pagan altars.

4 At night they go out among the graves,
worshiping the dead.
They eat the flesh of pigs
and make stews with other forbidden foods.

5 Yet they say to each other,
'Don't come too close or you will defile me!
I am holier than you!'
These people are a stench in my nostrils,
an acrid smell that never goes away.

6 "Look, my decree is written out in front of me:
I will not stand silent;
I will repay them in full!
Yes, I will repay them—

7 both for their own sins
and for those of their ancestors,"
says the Lord.

"For they also burned incense on the mountains
and insulted me on the hills.
I will pay them back in full!

8 "But I will not destroy them all," says the Lord.
"For just as good grapes are found
among a cluster of bad ones
(and someone will say,
'Don't throw them all away—
some of those grapes are good!'),
so I will not destroy all Israel.
For I still have true servants there.

9 I will preserve a remnant of the people of Israel
and of Judah to possess my land.
Those I choose will inherit it,
and my servants will live there.

10 The plain of Sharon will again be filled with flocks
for my people who have searched for me,
and the valley of Achor will
be a place to pasture herds.

11 "But because the rest of you have forsaken the Lord
and have forgotten his Temple,
and because you have prepared feasts to honor
the god of Fate
and have offered mixed wine to the god of Destiny,

12 now I will 'destine' you for the sword.
All of you will bow down before the executioner.
For when I called, you did not answer.
When I spoke, you did not listen.
You deliberately sinned—before my very eyes—
and chose to do what you know I despise."

¹³ Therefore, this is what
the Sovereign Lord says:
"My servants will eat,
but you will starve.
My servants will drink,
but you will be thirsty.
My servants will rejoice,
but you will be sad and ashamed.

¹⁴ My servants will sing for joy,
but you will cry in sorrow and despair.

¹⁵ Your name will be a curse word among my people,
for the Sovereign Lord will destroy you
and will call his true servants by another name.

¹⁶ All who invoke a blessing or take an oath
will do so by the God of truth.
For I will put aside my anger
and forget the evil of earlier days.

¹⁷ "Look! I am creating
new heavens and a new earth,
and no one will even think
about the old ones anymore.

¹⁸ Be glad; rejoice forever in my creation!
And look! I will create
Jerusalem as a place of happiness.
Her people will be a source of joy.

¹⁹ I will rejoice over Jerusalem
and delight in my people.
And the sound of weeping and crying
will be heard in it no more.

²⁰ "No longer will babies die
when only a few days old.
No longer will adults die before
they have lived a full life.
No longer will people be
considered old at one hundred!
Only the cursed will die that young!

²¹ In those days people will
live in the houses they build
and eat the fruit of their own vineyards.

²² Unlike the past, invaders will not take their houses
and confiscate their vineyards.
For my people will live as long as trees,
and my chosen ones will have time
to enjoy their hard-won gains.

²³ They will not work in vain,
and their children will
not be doomed to misfortune.
For they are people blessed by the Lord,
and their children, too, will be blessed.

²⁴ I will answer them before they even call to me.
While they are still talking about their needs,
I will go ahead and answer their prayers!

²⁵ The wolf and the lamb will feed together.
The lion will eat hay like a cow.
But the snakes will eat dust.
In those days no one will be hurt
or destroyed on my holy mountain.
I, the Lord, have spoken!"

66

¹ This is what the Lord says:
"Heaven is my throne, and the earth is my footstool.
Could you build me a temple as good as that?
Could you build me such a resting place?

² My hands have made both heaven and earth;
they and everything in them are mine.
I, the Lord, have spoken!
"I will bless those who have
humble and contrite hearts,
who tremble at my word.

³ But those who choose their own ways—
delighting in their detestable sins—
will not have their offerings accepted.
When such people sacrifice a bull,
it is no more acceptable than a human sacrifice.
When they sacrifice a lamb,
it's as though they had sacrificed a dog!
When they bring an offering of grain,
they might as well offer the blood of a pig.
When they burn frankincense,
it's as if they had blessed an idol.

⁴ I will send them great trouble—
all the things they feared.
For when I called, they did not answer.
When I spoke, they did not listen.

They deliberately sinned before my very eyes
and chose to do what they know I despise."

⁵ Hear this message from the Lord, all you who
tremble at his words: "Your own people hate you
and throw you out for being loyal to my name.
'Let the Lord be honored!' they scoff.
'Be joyful in him!'
But they will be put to shame.

⁶ What is all the commotion in the city?
What is that terrible noise from the Temple?
It is the voice of the Lord
taking vengeance against his enemies.

⁷ "Before the birth pains even begin,
Jerusalem gives birth to a son.

⁸ Who has ever seen anything as strange as this?
Who ever heard of such a thing?
Has a nation ever been born in a single day?
Has a country ever come forth in a mere moment?
But by the time Jerusalem's birth pains begin,
her children will be born.

⁹ Would I ever bring this nation to the point of birth
and then not deliver it?" asks the Lord.
"No! I would never keep
this nation from being born,"
says your God.

[10] "Rejoice with Jerusalem!
Be glad with her, all you who love her
and all you who mourn for her.
[11] Drink deeply of her glory
even as an infant drinks at its
mother's comforting breasts."
[12] This is what the Lord says:
"I will give Jerusalem a river
of peace and prosperity.
The wealth of the nations will flow to her.
Her children will be nursed at her breasts,
carried in her arms, and held on her lap.
[13] I will comfort you there in Jerusalem
as a mother comforts her child."
[14] When you see these things, your heart will rejoice.
You will flourish like the grass!
Everyone will see the Lord's hand of
blessing on his servants—
and his anger against his enemies.
[15] See, the Lord is coming with fire,
and his swift chariots roar like a whirlwind.
He will bring punishment with the fury of his anger
and the flaming fire of his hot rebuke.
[16] The Lord will punish the world by fire
and by his sword.
He will judge the earth,
and many will be killed by him.

[17] "Those who 'consecrate' and 'purify' themselves
in a sacred garden with its idol in the center—feasting
on pork and rats and other detestable meats—will
come to a terrible end," says the Lord. [18] "I can see
what they are doing, and I know what they are
thinking. So I will gather all nations and peoples
together, and they will see my glory. [19] I will perform
a sign among them. And I will send those who survive
to be messengers to the nations—to Tarshish, to the
Libyans and Lydians (who are famous as archers),
to Tubal and Greece, and to all the lands beyond
the sea that have not heard of my fame or seen my
glory. There they will declare my glory to the nations.
[20] They will bring the remnant of your people back
from every nation. They will bring them to my holy
mountain in Jerusalem as an offering to the Lord.
They will ride on horses, in chariots and wagons,
and on mules and camels," says the Lord. [21] "And I
will appoint some of them to be my priests and
Levites. I, the Lord, have spoken!

[22] "As surely as my new heavens and earth will remain,
so will you always be my people,
with a name that will never disappear,"
says the Lord.
[23] "All humanity will come to worship me
from week to week
and from month to month.
[24] And as they go out, they will see the dead bodies
of those who have rebelled against me.
For the worms that devour them will never die,
and the fire that burns them will never go out.
All who pass by
will view them with utter horror."

 ALABASTER

CO-FOUNDER, CREATIVE DIRECTOR
Bryan Ye-Chung

CO-FOUNDER, MANAGING DIRECTOR
Brian Chung

OPERATIONS DIRECTOR
Willa Jin

PRODUCT MANAGER
Tyler Zak

CONTENT EDITOR
Darin McKenna

COVER IMAGE
Carmen Leung

SPECIAL THANKS
Josephine Law, Original Designer

⬤ ALABASTER

CONTINUE THE CONVERSATION

www.alabasterco.com